A Family Affair

*How to Plan and Direct
the Best Family
Reunion Ever*

Sandra MacLean Clunies, CG

Amy Johnson Crow, CG
Series Editor

Rutledge Hill Press™
Nashville, Tennessee

A Division of Thomas Nelson, Inc.

Published by Rutledge Hill Press, a Division of Thomas Nelson, Inc., P.O. Box 141000, Nashville, Tennessee 37214.

The following items mentioned in this book are registered trademarks or service marks: About.com, American Family Immigration History Center, Ancestry.com, Anybirthday.com, Association for Gravestone Studies, Association of Professional Genealogists, AT&T's AnyWho, Board for Certification of Genealogists, CanadaGenWeb, CG, CGL, CGRS, Certified Genealogical Lecturer, Certified Genealogical Records Specialist, Certified Genealogist, ComeHome, Corel Paradox, Corel Quattro Pro, Creative Scrapbooking, Cyndi's List, Daughters of the American Revolution, Dogpile, Family Reunion Organizer (software), Family Tree Quilts (quilt-making service), FamilyBuzz.com, Fun Stuff for Genealogists, Genealogy.com, Get In Print, Google, Hanes, IBM, Infospace, International Business Machines, Internet-T-Shirts.com, Legacy (software), Logos2Promos, MapBlast, MapQuest, Marnex Products, MetaCrawler, Microsoft Access, Microsoft Excel, Microsoft Money, Microsoft PowerPoint, Minutiae Software, MyFamily.com, Office Depot, Outer Banks Lighthouse Society, ProFusion, Quicken, ReserveAmerica, Reunion Planner (software), Reunited! (software), RootsWeb, Scrapbooking.com, Social Security Death Index, Staples, Statue of Liberty-Ellis Island Foundation, Switchboard, TDC Games, The Master Genealogist, The Ultimates (telephone directory), Threads Unlimited, Tony Awards, USGenWeb, Visual Chartform, Whitepages.com, WorldGenWeb, Yahoo, Yahoo PeopleFind, Zip (hardware).

Library of Congress Cataloging-in-Publication Data

Clunies, Sandra MacLean.
    A family affair : how to plan and direct the best family reunion ever / Sandra MacLean Clunies.
       p. cm.—(National Genealogical Society guides)
    Includes index.
    ISBN 1-4016-0020-4 (pbk.)
    1. Family reunions—Planning. I. National Genealogical Society. II. Title. III. Series.
GT2423.C583 2003
394.2—dc21

2003007509

We each have families of chance, to whom we are biologically connected through the centuries. While we did not select our ancestors, many of us try to honor and give tribute to those who came before us by learning more about their lives and by understanding and appreciating their contribution to ourselves.

We also have families of choice—those people with whom we have freely chosen to establish a bond through marriage, adoption, or shared beliefs and values. Their experience, strength, and hope enrich and nourish our lives today.

This book is dedicated to all those special people, past and present, who—by chance or by choice—are cherished members of my family.

Contents

Acknowledgments

I AM GRATEFUL TO MANY FRIENDS, COLLEAGUES, AND E-MAIL CORRESPONDENTS, some of whom I have never met in person. By sharing their experiences, ideas, and permission to include their wisdom and Web sites, they helped me to reflect upon the larger family that supports us all. In alphabetical order by name, they are Ross Armer; Carrie Bodensteiner; Nedra Dickman Brill, CG; Dale Burkholder; Tony Burroughs; Douglas Campbell; Julia M. Case; Amy Johnson Crow, CG; James Derheim; Michael W. Donovan; Michelle Vardiman Fansler; Paul Giamona; Diana Hebner; Cyndi Howells; J. E. Jack; Eric James; Bobbi King; David Lee; Carole Leita; Mike Lenick; J. Mark Lowe, CG; Curtis Matthews, William Meacham; Eileen Polakoff; Pamela Boyer Porter, CGRS, CGL; Elissa Scalise Powell, CGRS; Barbara Renick; Beverly Rice, CGRS; Bruce Roberts; Cheryl Shelton Roberts; Bill Robey; Kevin Robidou; Richard Dennis Souther; Maureen A. Taylor; Sarah Walczynski; Terry White; Jim Windsor; Frank Wing; and Barbara Brixey Wylie.

INTRODUCTION

Who Should Read This Book?

"MY, HOW YOU'VE GROWN!" THAT'S THE GREETING I REMEMBER MOST as a child when we visited family members we didn't see often. Reunions—the coming together of extended families—may be regular events or rare ones. They can be small informal gatherings to celebrate a special milestone or large galas that draw dozens of folks from all over the world. Whatever the size, location, and focus, all family reunions share many of the same themes and dreams. They provide an opportunity for people to *be together*. And it takes just one special person to start the ball rolling—to turn a wish into reality.

Does the task seem large and overwhelming? When as a child I faced what seemed an impossible task, my grandmother would tell me I could eat an elephant if I cut it into bite-sized pieces. That's the trick. Take any large task, break it down into chewable chunks, and before you know it, you're done. If you've purchased this book, you are curious about what goes into planning a family reunion. Perhaps you've hesitated in the past because you simply didn't know how to do it. The help you need is here.

This book looks at the reunion as a theatrical production—after all, reunions also have many people working together backstage and onstage to produce a wonderful event for an appreciative audience who will join in on the fun. The chapters follow the steps you should take in planning and organizing this special production for your family. I suggest you skim through the chapter headings first and then sit down and read a chapter at a time. You'll find checklists and forms to help you simplify the paperwork,

1

tips from others who have held successful reunions, and plenty of references for further information on topics of special interest.

Here you have all the guidelines you need to make your family reunion an enjoyable experience in the planning stages and a memorable event for everyone. Now, on with the show!

Act 1
Production Design

CHAPTER 1

Backstage Brainstorming

What's a Reunion All About?

IT USED TO BE EASY TO FIND YOUR RELATIVES. EARLY IMMIGRANTS TO the American colonies often arrived in clusters of related groups, settled in one area, and could visit one another with little difficulty. Then some grown children set out to establish new settlements or they married a person from another community, sometimes far from home. After that, visiting became much more complicated.

When waves of immigrants began to arrive from Europe in the nineteenth century, people were sometimes separated from relatives and friends with whom they traveled. In our twenty-first century "global village," families are sometimes scattered so widely that entire branches lose touch with one another for years or generations. In fact, today we each tend to have several families—families of chance and families of choice. There are remarriages, blended families, single parents, partners, and significant others. Throughout this book, "family" refers to any person related to you through blood or marriage, or simply by choice.

Why Do Families Gather?

A woman called, seeking my services as a genealogist in her search for a missing brother. Since I don't specialize in searches for living people, I was planning to refer her to a colleague, but I asked a few questions first. She knew his name, his approximate birth date, and a state where he lived in the early 1980s, so I did two quick

Searching for Loved Ones

Thomas Paxton was born in Ireland in 1713 and emigrated to Pennsylvania. He lived to be over one hundred years old. His family spread out across the developing wilderness of the area, and tradition has it that Thomas was known to walk sixty miles to visit his children.

Immigrants in the nineteenth century scattered even more widely, and family members seeking to be reunited with their loved ones faced challenges greater than aching feet. Hoping to find long-lost relatives, Irish immigrants placed advertisements from 1831 to 1916 in the *Boston Pilot*, a newspaper with national circulation. The New England Historic Genealogical Society (NEHGS) has published seven volumes covering the period 1831–1876, entitled *The Search for Missing Friends: Irish Immigrant Advertisements Placed in the* Boston Pilot, and has released a CD of the same title, both edited by Ruth-Ann Harris and B. Emer O'Keefe. Here's an example:

Wanted of Maurice, John, Michael and Patrick Reding from the parish of Kilvert, county Cork, Ireland. In 1832 Patrick was in Baltimore. Any information respecting them will be tidings of joy to their brother Thomas, who now owns a farm in Leicester, Mass. [28 May 1842]

For more information about this resource, check out the NEHGS Web site at *www.newenglandancestors.org.*

searches on the Internet that gave two immediate clues. First, I confirmed that no man of his name and approximate age was listed in the Social Security Death Index *(ssdi.genealogy.rootsweb.com)*, an online database that lists persons whose beneficiaries collected Social Security benefits. That suggested he was still living. Second, with a search in The Ultimates *(www.theultimates.com)*, a comprehensive telephone directory database, I located three men of that name in that state. The database provided not only phone numbers, but also full street addresses. I suggested she try the phone numbers. Within the hour, she called back to say the first phone number was all she needed. She had talked for thirty minutes with her brother for the first time in twenty-five years—and a reunion would take place soon.

The U.S. Census Bureau reports continuous changes in the composition of households over the past century. From 1970 to 2000, the percentage of U.S. households composed of married couples with or without minor children decreased from 70.6 to 52.8, while the percentage of men and women living alone increased from 16.2 to 25.5. For more information about the changes in families and living arrangements, see the U.S. Census Web site at *factfinder.census.gov.*

Families come together to celebrate life's milestones and holidays. Births, marriages, birthdays, anniversaries, graduations, historical commemorations, and religious holidays are popular occasions for a family party. Where your ancestors may have gathered for a barn raising or harvest festival, today families gather to honor a retirement or a house-warming.

Since families in the past tended to remain in one geographical area for generations, going to grandmother's house was a familiar routine. Children attended the same schools as their parents, learned to swim in the same lake, and were married in the same chapel as many other family members. With families scattered far and wide today, children do not have those same experiences, so a reunion offers a way for parents to share their personal history: "Here's where I lived when I was your age." "Here's where I went to school." "This is where your great-grandparents are buried." Whether there is a special occasion to celebrate or you just want to visit with friends and relatives you don't often see, holding a reunion is a great way to bring people together.

The first international family-oriented reunion for children and grandchildren of Holocaust survivors took place in Chicago in 2002. "Living the Legacy" also included the first reunion of one thousand unaccompanied Jewish children who had been rescued from the Holocaust and brought to the United States between 1934 and 1945. To learn more, go to *chicago2002.descendants.org.*

What About a Theme?

As you see in Figure 1.1, the Burkholder family chose the theme "Coming Home" and met at their ancestral church of 1755. I attended one reunion of a family group celebrating the three hundred fiftieth anniversary of the mutual ancestor's arrival in America. Remarkably, there were still direct descendants living on that saltwater farm in Massachusetts.

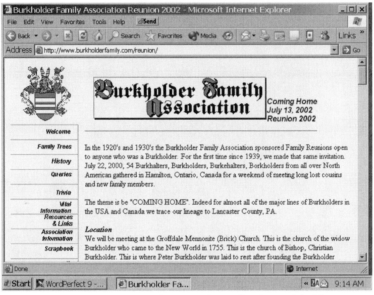

Figure 1.1 "Coming Home," the 2002 theme for the Burkholder Family Reunion

At a reunion of my own family, we arranged to have a special ceremony to honor a Revolutionary War ancestor by placing a Daughters of the American Revolution marker at his grave site. It happened that three female descendants were DAR members in three different states; together, they arranged the special tribute. Children served as a color guard, carrying the American flag. Two descendants who are professional musicians contributed beautiful renditions of the national anthem and taps. The life story of the ancestor was read aloud, and the reunion materials included a commemorative booklet. Figure 1.2 shows the cover of the booklet.

Lots of imaginative ideas can be developed for a reunion, and creating a theme for the event is a great way to interest people. One friend plans to take her mother back to her birthplace in Ireland to celebrate the mother's ninetieth birthday. She has arranged

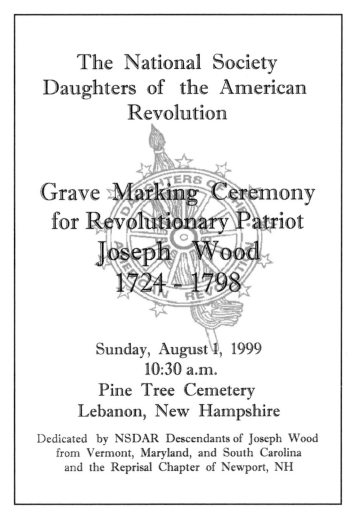

The National Society
Daughters of the American
Revolution

Grave Marking Ceremony
for Revolutionary Patriot
Joseph Wood
1724 - 1798

Sunday, August 1, 1999
10:30 a.m.
Pine Tree Cemetery
Lebanon, New Hampshire

Dedicated by NSDAR Descendants of Joseph Wood
from Vermont, Maryland, and South Carolina
and the Reprisal Chapter of Newport, NH

Figure 1.2 Cover of the commemorative booklet presented as part of the DAR grave-marking ceremony at one Wood Reunion

a surprise gathering of friends and family in "the old country"—an old-fashioned birthday tea party. Another family I know holds an annual "Cousins Invitational," an informal golf tournament at which non-golfing family members either trail the players as a cheering gallery or remain at the picnic site to help prepare the festive meal. Other themes you might consider for your own reunion include the wedding anniversary of a shared ancestor, the date a pioneer couple first settled in a community, and the birth of a great-grandchild—celebrating four living generations.

"One Plate, One Spoon," a 1640s dinner, was one feature of the Wing Family of America Inc.'s one hundredth consecutive reunion in 2002. Family members were encouraged to dress in their "1640s duds" for the reunion theme "Seeing Our Past—Facing Our Future."

What Kind of Show Should It Be?

There are lots of things to consider when planning a reunion: What style might your family prefer? A casual picnic in the park? A week aboard a cruise ship? Both price and personal preferences help you decide what kind of reunion event will work for your family. You'll need to think about a number of planning issues—let's call it *backstage brainstorming*.

Setting the Scope

You have two basic family trees to climb—your mother's and your father's. In many families, one side is larger, more well known, or better connected than the other. Perhaps you already know all your first cousins on one or both sides of your family. Is that the size of the group you envision getting together? Or do you want to extend it back in time a generation or two or more—to meet second cousins or third cousins? Perhaps you want to include all descendants of a particular ancestral couple, which often means cousins by the dozens. To keep it simple, you may want to take one family tree at a time.

When an extended family gathers, it can be confusing to sort out just how everyone is related. For one reunion, I created a chart (see Figure 1.3) that clearly presents the "cousin connections." You might want to adapt it to help you decide just how many cousins you'll be inviting.

The Wood Work

My maternal grandmother was born in 1876 in New Hampshire to a family named Wood. She was one of fourteen children, and the family expanded each generation. Researching her ancestry, I found that her great-great-grandparents left Connecticut in 1766 to become original settlers of a new town in the undeveloped New Hampshire

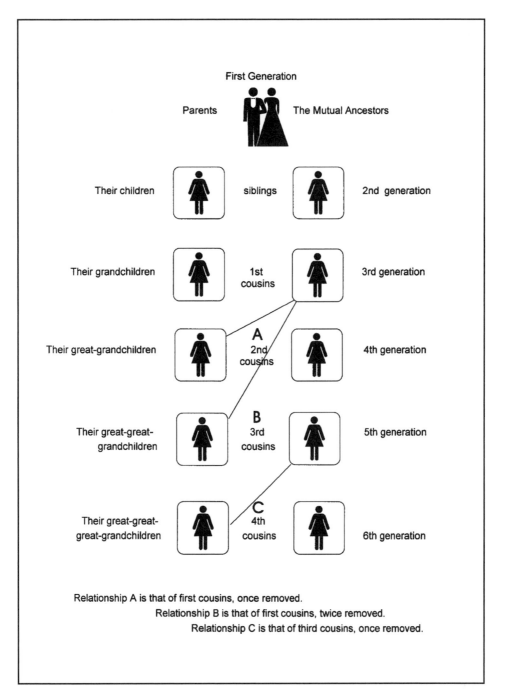

Figure 1.3 The cousin connections chart

Figure 1.4 My mother and her grandfather at a 1911 reunion

wilderness. Parents of twelve children, they had eighty-three grandchildren. I decided to track the living descendants of this couple—Joseph and Anna (Palmer) Wood—and have a family reunion.

I knew the names and addresses of two of my mother's surviving first cousins who still lived in that area. And I was lucky—I had some historical help. As a child, my mother had attended a 1911 reunion to celebrate her grandfather's eightieth birthday. Photographs were taken on that special day, and Jeremiah Wood took some time away from the larger crowd to pose with his young granddaughter, who was all dressed up for the occasion (see Figure 1.4). I refer to this reunion project, which I call the "Wood Work" throughout this book as an example of my own reunion-planning experiences.

Ballpark or Ballroom?

The only limits to planning the type of event your family will enjoy are your imagination—and your budget. To keep the costs per family member to a reasonable rate and to encourage regular attendance, the best approach is to hold an informal gathering near a relative's home area. "Special occasion" reunions call for a more elaborate, elegant, or expensive scenario. You'll find ideas about reunion locations in Chapter 3, but here are a few options to consider early on:

- **Neighborhood**
  - Near a family member's home
    - Potluck backyard picnic (This requires a big backyard.)
    - Cookout at a local park, fairgrounds, or community center
    - Banquet at a hotel or restaurant

- **Out of Town**
  - Away from home
    - Favorite beach
    - Mountain resort
    - Dude ranch
    - Theme park
  - Train trip to
    - National park
    - Historic site with activities, such as Colonial Williamsburg
  - Afloat
    - Houseboat
    - Cruise ship
    - Canoe trip
    - Steamboat
    - Abroad
    - Trip to the original homeland of immigrant ancestors

If this is your first reunion, keep it simple: Plan an event that is available to and affordable for the majority of family members you want to attend. A picnic or cookout at a public park or community center is the easiest to arrange, as long as you have covered pavilions or a back-up indoor location in case the weather gremlins pull a surprise on you.

Invite Everyone

If your family is typical, not everyone feels close to everyone else. Aunt Mary won't come to an event if her husband's brother Henry is going to appear, because Mary has never forgiven Henry for something that happened twenty years ago. I encourage you to avoid falling into the trap of deciding who should or shouldn't be invited. Invite everyone, and if some people choose not to attend lest they meet up with an estranged relative, that's their choice. You should prepare an event at which everyone is welcome—with enough variety and space so that no one will be required to interact with or sit next to any particular person. Who knows? Perhaps fences will be mended and relationships restored—it's happened before.

Some family members will have absolutely no interest in meeting as a large family group, for a variety of personal reasons. Don't become discouraged if a few doors seem to slam in your face as you begin. Theirs is not a personal rebuff—it simply reflects the priorities and privacy needs of that person or family group. The first reunion I organized had several "holdouts"—including some who heard later about the fun everyone had and signed up early for the next one.

Ask the Audience!

Communication is key to a successful reunion, from the earliest planning stages to the post-reunion follow-up. So consider taking a tip from successful marketing research strategists. Before a new product or project is launched, companies often use "focus groups" to sample the potential customers; in informal discussions, participants contribute their ideas about what they want in the proposed new product. Why not survey a few of your closest family members about reunion ideas and get some feedback early on? Apart from getting some useful ideas from other family members, there's another benefit: They feel involved. That means they are much more likely to encourage others near them to participate, as well.

Start Early

Planning a reunion means starting at least a year ahead—eighteen months to two years is even better if you want to meet at a popular location. Keep in mind that many families make their vacation plans far in advance and children today often have busy summer schedules with camps and activities. This means that if you are considering a summer reunion, you should begin to ask people about their ideas at least as early as the spring of the year before. You may know someone who once arranged a fancy wedding in a few weeks, but that is certainly not the common or comfortable way to handle a big event. Planning takes time. The more research you do, the more you enhance your options and opportunities.

There are many checklists and timetables throughout this book to help you organize your steps at each stage of your production. They offer suggestions, which you should adapt to the special needs and wishes of your own audience.

Send It Out

Another way to gather ideas and to interest others in the actual planning is to contact a select list of relatives by mail. All you need is a cover letter that presents the idea and a form to be returned. Figures 1.5 and 1.6 show examples of a cover letter and survey form designed to send to relatives you've met before. Some readers tend to put aside surveys, even family ones, and then never get around to sending them. So to increase the response rate, include a self-addressed stamped envelope (SASE). (Be sure to keep track of all these

---

Dear Evelyn,

What do you think about holding a Wood Family Reunion next year? It's been over fifty years since the descendants of Joseph and Anna (Palmer) Wood last gathered together in New Hampshire. Cousins Bob Cutler and Alice Johnson came by recently, and we talked about it a lot. We all thought about you, and want to know how you feel about it.

Where and when should we hold it? What kind of event do you think would be best? How could you help?

I enclose a survey for you to fill out and return to me so we can move forward with preliminary planning for a reunion everyone will enjoy! You can also phone or e-mail me, if that's more convenient.

Even if you're not sure whether you could attend, we'd really value your thoughts and ideas. I'll let everyone know the results of our "brainstorming," and the next steps we can take to turn this wish into a reality.

Sincerely,

My name
My address
My phone number
My fax
My e-mail address

Figure 1.5 Sample cover letter to relatives

Survey About a Wood Family Reunion

Name: _____

Any change in address? _____

Phone:_____ e-mail: _____

Interest in a family reunion: __ yes!   __ maybe   __don't think so

Best date for my family (please rank proposed dates):
__ June   __July   __ August   __1st weekend __2nd __3rd __4th

Other best date for me: _____

Preferred type: __ picnic/cookout in park   __hotel/restaurant   __ a family home

Length: __ one day   __ weekend

Other idea for type _____

Number of people in my immediate family:

____adults ____children 10 and over ___children 9 and under

__ I'd be willing to help out in the following ways:

__ serve on a committee   __head up a committee __help out onsite

Other: _____

Other cousins who might want to know about and help with ideas for the reunion:

Name: _____
Address: _____
Phone: _____ e-mail : _____

Name : _____
Address: _____
Phone: _____ e-mail: _____

Please return to: [*My name and address*]

Figure 1.6 Sample survey form

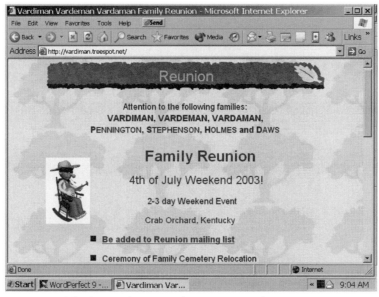

Figure 1.7 The banjo-playing Vardiman Reunion logo

initial expenses, such as postage and long-distance phone calls. Once you create the budget—see Chapter 4—perhaps these start-up costs can be reimbursed.)

Did you notice the graphic art at the top of the survey form? This is a logo I have used since the very beginning of the Wood Work. The colonial town crier alludes to our ancestors who lived in colonial America. It became a "signature" for the project, and I use it on newsletters, return address labels, and other publicity materials. In Figure 1.7, you see that the Vardiman family uses a country banjo player logo to highlight its Kentucky reunion. On the Vardiman Web site, banjo music accompanies the theme.

E-mail It

I know people who would never take the time to sit down and write a letter, address it, stamp it, and take it to a mailbox, but give these same people the one-stop speed and convenience of e-mail, and they often become active correspondents! You can use e-mail to great advantage in your reunion planning, for ease of both communication and organization. For instance, you can set up special folders in which to keep messages pertaining to the reunion. And creating a new group in your address book particularly for the reunion is an efficient way to send e-mails to several people at once. But be sure to keep e-mail address changes updated to avoid that dreaded "not deliverable" error message.

If someone in your inner circle is Web savvy, you may want to plan for a family Web site—more about that in Chapter 7.

What to Ask

Whether you contact other relatives in person or by phone, mail, or e-mail, have a standard set of questions prepared. That way, you'll get the same level of replies from everyone you contact. For instance, be sure to cover these basics:

- Are you interested in a family reunion?
- When and where do you think it should be held?
- What type of event do you prefer?
- Do you know others to contact about planning the reunion?
- Are you willing to help?

Warm Up on Cold Calls

Marketing folks use the term "cold call" to describe first contact with people who don't expect a letter or call and whom you've never met before. Think about all the unwelcome cold calls you receive by phone, fax, and mail from aggressive salespersons or inappropriate organizations. Which ones get your attention? That's one way to think about how to make successful cold calls to distant relatives and how to start a positive conversation with cousins you may never have met.

Whatever the method of communication, your goal is to interest others in attending the reunion. Therefore, initial contacts should be friendly, simple—and brief. Too much information up front may turn off your listener and derail what you want to hear: a simple expression of possible interest. Discussing obligations of cost or other commitments too early may discourage a positive response.

Figure 1.5 showed you a sample letter to send out to relatives you already know. What about people you have never met? How do you introduce yourself to Cousin Michael in Maine? If you have a phone number, chances are that you got it from another relative known to Michael, and a phone call can begin with that connection:

Hello, Michael. Margaret Nelson gave me your name and number. This is Sandy Clunies, and I'm a cousin of yours on your father's side. Your grandfather George Wood and my grandmother Josie Wood were brother and sister.

For a mailing, you might change the first paragraph of the letter in Figure 1.5 to read:

Hello! I am sending this to many cousins I have never met, so let me introduce myself. I am a great-granddaughter of Jeremiah (1831–1918) and Martha (Dickinson) Wood of West Lebanon, New Hampshire. There used to be large family reunions of the Wood family, but the last one was over fifty years ago. What do you think about holding a Wood Family Reunion next year?

Talk It Over in Person

Market researchers know that group settings generate more ideas than surveys or one-on-one conversations because people stimulate one another to participate. So why not gather a few folks at another family event—the next holiday meal or big birthday party—and ask for suggestions? At the next graduation or wedding, mention a few reunion ideas to get the conversation started.

Join the Team

A reunion needs lots of helpers, and this first stage of backstage planning lets you know which relatives may be available to help. Even if volunteers live far from the reunion site, they can do a number of things long distance to help during the preparation phase of the reunion. For instance, you might ask each branch of the family to consider a five-minute presentation during the reunion to showcase some of their talents and contributions. Chapter 2 presents more details on "auditions" for the cast and crew, but your very first meetings will likely turn up a few good candidates.

Write It Down

Even during an informal chat, have a pad of paper on hand to write down all the good ideas. Better yet, get a simple three-ring binder and you'll have started on the record-keeping tasks, too. Note the names of everyone and the ideas they propose or support.

Name	Date Met	Date Phoned	Date Survey Mailed	Notes and Next Steps

Figure 1.8 Sample log used to track contacts

You'll find lots more about record keeping in Chapter 5 and throughout this book, but it starts now. How will you keep track of all those you've contacted? Figure 1.8 shows a sample form you can use for starters.

Automate the Paperwork

It's no secret that one of the best uses of a computer is to keep records. Perhaps you already use databases in many aspects of your work or personal business. If so, you know their value. If not, you will soon come to appreciate them.

Commercial software programs have been created specifically to handle a reunion, but you can also create your own record-keeping system in spreadsheet or database programs that are often bundled with new computers, such as Microsoft Excel, Microsoft Access, Corel Quattro Pro, and Corel Paradox. When I held my first large family reunion in 1994, all I had were my word processor and a financial program. So I know firsthand that another option is to create simple databases on your computer with tables and sorting functions. Chapter 5 offers detailed descriptions and suggestions to help you establish a useful record-keeping system.

Survey Results

As you record the survey replies, begin to sort them into "yes" and "maybe" groups. At this point, don't count out all of those who may have said "no" to the first contact. If they took the time to talk with you or send a reply, they are still possible participants and helpers. The challenge is to convert those who replied "don't think so" to an enthusiastic "count me in!"

Now is a good time to pause and measure your progress with a timetable of steps. Production Timetable 1, shown in Figure 1.9, shows you the first level of a timetable—the planning that should be accomplished one to two years before your reunion takes place. Once you've had a few preliminary talks or meetings with family members and received feedback from the survey, you're ready to move on to bigger decisions and audition the cast and crew for the "big show."

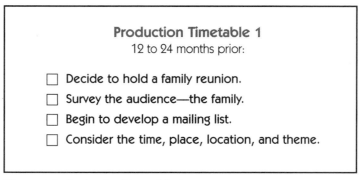

Figure 1.9 Production Timetable 1

CHAPTER 2

Casting Call

Auditions for the Cast and Crew

THINK OF ALL THE CATEGORIES THAT ARE HONORED AT THE TONY Awards. Every great production depends on both team effort and the individual work of skilled backstage people. When the award winners give those acceptance speeches, they usually have a long list of other lesser-known names to thank. From the set designers to the hairdressers, from the choreographer to the wardrobe staff, dozens of tributes are paid to those who made the performance possible. While the onstage performers may be the most visible, it's the crew backstage that deserves most of the credit.

Scout within your extended family for people who can take on a variety of jobs to make your reunion a smooth and successful production. Let's examine some of these jobs.

The Producer

The producer has many roles: planner, advisor, team builder, manager, and partnership builder. The producer should have a group of others to handle a number of the production tasks, but for a small reunion, many activities may rest on the producer's shoulders. Let's look at what this essential person does.

Planner

Many large and small organizations develop a mission statement—a brief description of goals and objectives that serve as a guide to the work. It describes the purpose, the reason for the organization's existence, and the shared values of the group—and does so in a way that inspires support and ongoing commitment. The mission statement drives what businesses call "strategic planning." Figure 2.1 shows what the Robidou family has developed for its reunions.

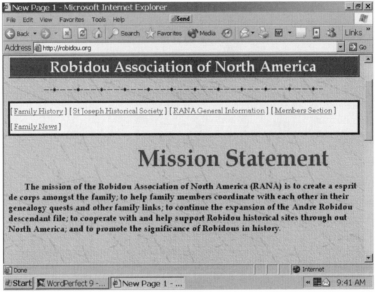

Figure 2.1 A family organization's mission statement

Creating a mission statement is a fine first step for planning a family reunion. Try to develop your mission statement in a group setting; those many and diverse views all need to be heard. "We want to have a good time." "We want to expand our bonds with family groups." "We want to honor the ancestors." "We want the children to know their personal heritage." The producer can facilitate this discussion and help the group come to a consensus that is articulated in a few sentences.

The mission statement provides the vision and thus the foundation; all planning and the successful production itself builds from that base—including the events and activities that can support the vision, within the budgets and time constraints acknowledged in those few sentences. Time spent on the mission statement up front in your planning process is well rewarded.

Advisor

As the reunion team's work progresses, the producer advises in many ways, from providing "lessons learned" during previous reunions to managing the varying opinions about site selection, time, events, and other issues. Remember, however, that an advisor is not a dictator—the advisor suggests ideas and solutions but doesn't demand or order others around. The producer as advisor is a mentor or coach, helping others to succeed in their assignments.

Team Builder

We should look to successful businesses in the area of team building, a tool designed to improve productivity, communication, and working relationships. Your team for the reunion may be far-flung, with members located at a physical distance from one another. But teams make sense whether your meetings are conducted in Uncle Arnie's family room or over the Internet in an e-mail group.

Working as a team means involving all the appropriate people in decision making. It means asking questions and listening carefully to the responses of each team member. The best results come when different opinions and ideas surface in meetings. That one innovative suggestion may just be a new way to work through a problem area.

A team builder should expect resistance and mistakes—and the unexpected. A healthy sense of humor goes a long way in making others feel comfortable. As a team builder, the

Team-Building Tips
- Take time to inform and validate others.
- Expect mistakes and the unexpected.
- Allow all to contribute.
- Make it fun—laugh together!

producer should value the individual strengths and differences among team members, and give them the information, resources, and support to accomplish their work.

Manager

A manager has lots of tasks: directing, supervising, coordinating, assessing, implementing, educating, facilitating, leading, and more. You know you can do some tasks better than you can do others. Good managers share one trait: They have an honest view of their own strengths and limitations. A big part of managing a reunion is knowing when to delegate. One of my own limitations is that I don't *delegate* enough; I end up *doing* too much of the work myself. Fortunately, I have learned from observing others at work what management techniques work best for me. Most of all, the manager should remember: delegate, delegate, delegate.

Partnership Builder

People and organizations outside your family group have an impact on the success of your reunion. You will create several partnerships with other entities during the reunion organization. For instance, site selection requires working with those responsible for reservations at a given location. If you choose to have a caterer provide the meals, you will work with that business as well. To add information to your family history, you may work with historical societies or genealogists. The key elements to all partnerships are *collaboration* and *cooperation*.

The Wood family ancestors were early settlers of Lebanon, New Hampshire, so during my reunion planning, I worked extensively with the local town historian. He was a treasure trove of information, providing details on the family that none of us knew. We invited him to make a presentation at the 1994 reunion and again in 1999. He suggested tours of the town to see old family residences and even served as a guide.

Since I am a Certified Genealogist, I offered to work with him on extending his own family tree, and we were both delighted to discover that he had a distinct link to our Wood family himself through earlier mutual ancestors. At the 1999 reunion, I presented him with a laminated wall chart of his ancestry in gratitude for our wonderfully productive partnership.

Is producer the part that you will play? Or will another family member assume this role? The producer is the person ultimately responsible for the whole show and must have some special qualities: commitment to the project, organizational skills, and the ability to communicate with others.

Commitment to the Project

It takes vision, dedication, and persistence—the components of commitment—to guide a reunion. In addition to having a clear understanding of the goals of the event and a vision of the paths to take to accomplish those goals, the producer must demonstrate both commitment to and belief in the project. After all, every project has its pitfalls—those unforeseen or unexpected difficulties that challenge planners and managers. The caterer you hired in December goes out of business in May, a month before your reunion. Can you find another in a hurry? Or will you shift gears and quickly organize a potluck meal with donations from families? The producer remains calm during these little surprise storms and seeks creative solutions to the challenges—always with an eye on the goal.

Organizational Skills

In a way, the producer is the reunion team's leader. The person who takes on this task should excel at what is today called "multitasking,"—the ability to juggle a variety of tasks at the same time. Save your "specialists" for key team assignments.

Many separate activities come together to ensure the success of a reunion—including the mailings, the meals, and the meetings. Remember the old vaudeville act that featured a person balancing spinning plates atop a pole? After getting the first plate spinning, he would quickly move to start a second whirling, and then a third, and on down the line. As one plate began to wobble, the performer would dash back to that pole and get that plate spinning smoothly again. A successful producer keeps all the plates spinning.

Good leaders supervise and delegate tasks to others and then provide the support that enables others to make their best contributions. In a pinch, the producer can step in and pick up some loose ends, so it's important that this person understands all the roles and their responsibilities.

Ability to Communicate with Others

Can you listen well to what others are saying? Listening is a major strength in effective communication. Can you also get your own message across in a way that is easily understood by others? Look at Figure 2.2. Has this ever happened to you? It is an amusing way to describe what many of us experience in conversations every day. Great thoughts and ideas can be lost forever unless the speaker and the listener confirm that they both hear and understand the same message. When several people are exchanging information at a team meeting, it is helpful to sometimes pause and consider what you *think* you heard.

> *I know you believe you understand what you think I said, but what you heard is not what I meant.*

Figure 2.2 Communication challenges

Successful leaders take time to respect and value the communications they receive from others on their team. They encourage participation from everyone at a meeting, not just the outspoken few. It is more effective to build consensus than to control. A team leader should summarize group discussions and provide feedback to be sure that everyone is singing from the same songbook.

The producer's success is related directly to the extent to which he or she provides a variety of ways to communicate with team members. Some will respond to phone calls but never read memos. Others will find phone calls disruptive and prefer to read instructions; still others will respond best in a face-to-face meeting.

The Business Manager

The next important job is business manager or treasurer, for which a number of skills come into play:

- Experience in creating and managing budgets

- Experience in keeping financial records

- Ability to negotiate contracts (optional)

Experience in Creating and Managing Budgets

Each of us has some experience with budgets; it would be hard to run a household without some idea of the amount of money coming in and going out. The business manager does not have to be the chief financial officer of a major corporation to do a fine job for the family reunion. The budget will be created as a group effort of the planning team, and the business manager will then implement it. If your family is large, perhaps a finance team with the business manager as its head will better suit your needs. The primary traits needed for this task include having a realistic view of income and expense categories, and being able to propose changes or adjustments as the planning proceeds and new information is acquired. More specific details about budget management appear in Chapter 4.

Tracking Costs and Reporting

Our ancestors may have kept the "egg money" in a sugar bowl, and some of your family members may still manage their finances with little more than a checkbook and a pocket calculator. The business manager/treasurer is responsible for the finances and accountable for all funds received and disbursed, and should have signature privileges on the reunion checking account. In addition, the business manager

- Promptly deposits all money received

- Tracks all income and expenses

- Monitors expenses against budget

- Regularly reports to the production team and, through them, to the audience in mailings or newsletters

- Makes a final financial statement after all reunion income has been received and expenses have been paid

It is helpful, though not essential, that the person who takes the role of business manager for your production have not only financial record-keeping experience but also knowledge of a personal finance software program, such as Quicken or Microsoft Money. Not only does such a program simplify the record-keeping task, but it also enables easy reporting. In Quicken, for example, you can print out the following items: income and expense comparison reports and graphs, itemized categories reports, budget reports and variance graphs, banking summary reports, missing checks reports, and cash flow reports. And the visual graphs are often much easier to understand than numerical reports. Of course, it's always possible that the best person available for the job of business manager doesn't happen to use a computer program and will keep records in a handwritten ledger book. In this case, the planning team needs to decide how important it is to have a candidate familiar with computers for the position.

Ability to Negotiate Contracts

"But you said you would have containers with ice to hold the soft drinks," you say to the caterer who arrives at the reunion site with cases of warm soda. "No, you said you would provide those," he replies. Oral agreements, although friendly, can be misunderstood, hazardous, and uncontrollable. Written contracts provide customer protection. When you make arrangements with a vendor or facility to provide particular goods or services at a certain price, you should have a contract that clearly spells out *all* the details. Leave nothing to interpretation. Most hotels, conference centers, public parks that rent space, and other similar facilities have standard contract forms. But an individual organization, like your reunion group, can always lobby for changes and additions that best meet the needs of your group.

The business manager should be well versed in details in order to negotiate comprehensive contracts. While the entire reunion team may want to chime in on what items should be included, the person who signs the contract is ultimately responsible for what goes into it.

Chapter 4 discusses the "money matters" critical to your show's success and goes into detail about contracts.

The Record Keeper

From the first name and phone number you jotted down on the back of an envelope when this idea for a reunion bloomed in your mind, you have begun the record keeping. But those records need to shift from scraps of paper to a safe and sane system so you can track all the many details of the show. Whether you've inherited a box full of index cards from previous reunions or Aunt Mary's tattered address book of distant relatives, your mailing list should be converted to an online database or upgraded to a usable paper system.

The record keeper must be organized, with a flair for frequent updating as new information is received, and must also be a team player who works well with others assigned to different tasks. Everyone needs to know what the record keeper knows, so each person knows where to go for information. The record keeper maintains the mailing list as it develops, and also helps create and mail the announcements, registration forms, and reminders. The record keeper may also be the person who submits news of the reunion to local newspapers, online reunion registries, and other publicity sources.

Several new computer software programs are specifically designed to handle the details of large group events like reunions. Trial versions can be downloaded from the Internet to see whether they meet your needs before you purchase them. You'll learn more about record keeping in Chapter 5.

The record keeper is an integral part of the production team; be sure the person assigned to this role gets all the assistance, support, and supplies needed to do the job.

The Stage Manager

What's the script for the reunion show? How will the day, weekend, or week play out? What will happen at what time and where? Arranging for all the different events, gathering supplies or "props," staging the "acts"—and managing a crew, of sorts—is the stage manager's job. These important tasks help the event move smoothly from beginning to end, so you want an outgoing and creative person to take on this assignment. Here are some of the crew members the stage manager must oversee:

- **Set designer/decorator:** Works with the facility regarding space arrangements, tables and chairs, and other equipment, and leads the set-up team.

- **Recorder:** Supervises video and still cameras.

- **Sound director:** Arranges for DJ, tape recordings, microphones, and speakers.

- **Art/visual effects director:** Assists the set designer with genealogy charts, signs, and other visual displays.

- **Costume designer:** Arranges for reunion T-shirts, caps, and costumes for skits.

- **Continuity editor:** Usually the family historian or genealogist; collects family information and works with the art director to produce charts, displays, and other publications such as memory books.

Teams

Producer, business manager, record keeper, stage manager—these four persons are the key decision makers and problem solvers of the reunion planning team. Their work is the foundation for your whole production. With strong leadership and financial responsibility, you're on your way to a sell-out smash event.

While assigning these key roles, you should also think about what kinds of support teams you need to create. How you choose to set up the overall reunion team depends, of course, on your decisions about the type of event you want to put on. But these are the areas you will probably need to assign to smaller, specific teams:

- Adult activities (supervision, supplies, and prizes)
- Children's activities (supervision, supplies, and prizes)
- Door prizes and "goodie bags" (purchased prizes, merchant and family donations, personalized gifts, and the bags)
- Lodging arrangements (hotels and campgrounds)
- Transportation (airport pick-ups, buses between locations, and parking lot guides)
- Refreshments (food, whether potluck, catered, or supplied by a facility)
- Registration desk (name tags, badges, sign in, and raffle tickets)
- Special events (auction, raffle, church service, memorial service, golf tournament, scholarship award, and side trips for out-of-town visitors)

A detailed discussion of each of these teams and their roles and responsibilities appears in later chapters. This introduction to your necessary cast and crew is intended to start you thinking about which people can best serve in these roles. If you expect your reunion to have fewer than fifty attendees, then probably one person can assume more than one role in the cast. You might let volunteers choose the parts they want to play. If you don't get enough volunteers the first time around, approach specific persons for specific jobs. Sometimes folks are just too bashful to volunteer, but will help when asked by someone who shows confidence in them.

The producer and the stage manager work closely with most of the teams. Once the budget and finances have been established, the business manager will become a key consultant to all teams that have expenditures.

Team Communications and Conflicts

Clear and continuous communications among team members is essential, especially when they live hundreds of miles from one another. The best way to ensure this is e-mail; the next best is telephone conferences. However you communicate, all meetings and conferences should be documented and summarized for all members. It's too easy to forget details or assignments in the excitement of planning. And if more than two people are on the line during a conference call, it can be confusing to remember who said what. After a phone conference or any other meeting, the record keeper should write down the summary and circulate it to make sure everyone understood the same thing.

Group meetings inherently have the potential for misunderstandings and personality conflicts. Such difficulties can happen anywhere, but sometimes escalate in family groups. Uncle Fred insists there is only one way to do anything—his way. On general principles, Cousin Jim always disagrees with Uncle Fred. Whatever Aunt Jane chooses is likely to be voted down by Aunt Eleanor, who thinks Jane is frivolous and wastes money. Who's the referee when family disagreements threaten your peace and plans? While it's the producer's role to move things along, reaching consensus is always the goal. The producer should take the following steps to keep the peace:

- Review all the positions on which there *is* agreement before dealing with individual points of disagreement.

- Focus on the long-term goals of a successful reunion and work toward mutual resolutions.

- Try to acknowledge and examine mistakes without making personal attacks.

- Seek solutions rather than blaming someone on the team.

You can find tips on building consensus on the Web at *www.funteambuilding.com* and *humanresources.about.com/library/weekly/aa112501b.htm*.

You've now assembled a stellar cast and crew to plan and produce your family reunion. There will be a script to plan, lines to learn, and rehearsals before the big opening day.

Check your progress with Production Timetable 2, shown in Figure 2.3, and then let's move on to the next phase of the production design—selecting the right time and the right place.

Production Timetable 2
12 to 24 months prior:

☑ Decide to hold a family reunion.
☑ Survey the audience—the family.
☑ Begin to develop a mailing list.
☑ Consider the time, place, location, and theme.
☐ Hold auditions for the cast and crew.
☐ Select the producer and the business manager.

Figure 2.3 Production Timetable 2

CHAPTER 3

The Right Time . . . the Right Place

When Is Showtime?

Next Year, or the Year After

IF I HAD TO GIVE JUST ONE PIECE OF ADVICE ABOUT PLANNING A FAMILY reunion, it would be this: Plan ahead. Give yourself at least a year. Even two years in advance is not too soon to start planning for a major reunion, so get out the calendars. For a first reunion, keep the planning as simple as you can. Most families take time off during the summer months to travel, especially those with school-aged children. So the months of July and August are very good candidates.

A small group with common interests might opt for a different time of year—skiers need snow, for example. A visit to a Florida theme park is more comfortable outside the hot summer months. Location may also figure into your decision. Weekend discounts are available at many hotels that cater to weekday business travelers, and you can find similar discounts at most resorts during the off-season.

Since many popular gathering places require reservations a year in advance, if you have a particular location in mind, that may determine the date of your event—especially if you are renting a facility. But the popularity of a location may limit you to certain dates, even if you choose free spots such as local and state parks. Check with the agencies or authorities that manage particular facilities for guidelines on how early to make reservations.

Consider the weather in selecting a reunion location. On 26 June 1990 in Phoenix, Arizona, the temperature was 122 degrees Fahrenheit. On 23 January 1971 in Prospect Creek, Alaska, the temperature was minus 80 degrees Fahrenheit.

Linking with Other Events: Pro and Con

Some families schedule a reunion time to coincide with another event happening in the selected area. Beware of the pitfalls if you do this. For instance, selecting Washington, D.C., on the Fourth of July would certainly provide a host of activities and entertainment for everyone. But traffic jams and the challenge of keeping track of people in a crowd of hundreds of thousands would be a distinct downside. In rural communities, the annual county fair is often a big event. Perhaps family members are active in the associations that sponsor or participate in the fair. Gathering a family audience to cheer on Cousin Bob in the competition for best in show for his champion rabbits, roses, or rhubarb pie would provide a family focus to a community event. But the same considerations about parking and hotel space apply to large rural events, where there may be even fewer options available.

County fairs and local festivals often draw quite a crowd, which can make hotel rooms scarce—as do college reunions! After we had confirmed the dates for one Wood reunion in New Hampshire, we found out that on the same weekend we'd selected, nearby Dartmouth College was holding a parents weekend. It came as a total surprise, as we'd picked a July weekend, and never expected that the college would hold a major event at that time. It meant strong competition for local hotel rooms, and we had to advise our group to reserve early to avoid disappointment.

So if you want to explore the possibilities of linking up with other events scheduled in a given area, check the community newspapers or look for a Web site that lists coming events—and then start dialing for hotel rooms.

You can also use your reunion to create a community event, as some families have done by rededicating a family cemetery or planting memorial trees. Such an event will generate additional publicity for your reunion. For example, at a family reunion in Quebec, a commemorative plate was installed on the wall of the church where the mutual ancestors had married in 1690.

Over the years, as reunions become established, a certain weekend is often set as a standard time—the second weekend of August, for example. Whether the group meets each year or every three or five years, everyone knows when the next one will be. Remember, though, that no single date will ever accommodate every person's schedule, so expect an occasional conflict of interest. And once you set a date, stick with it. Otherwise, all your valuable time will be spent negotiating calendars.

Places Everyone!

Deciding on the location for your reunion is one of the first things you will do—and that decision will drive the "ticket prices" for the show. The Souther Family 2005 reunion in Hawaii has been publicized years in advance with a comprehensive and colorful Web site. In Figure 3.1, you see announcements in 2002 and, in Figure 3.2, an attractive graphic adds to the anticipation.

Aim for the location that is most accessible and affordable to the majority of those people you want to attend. What's the attraction to them? Will the journey be as enjoyable as the destination? Here are some issues to consider:

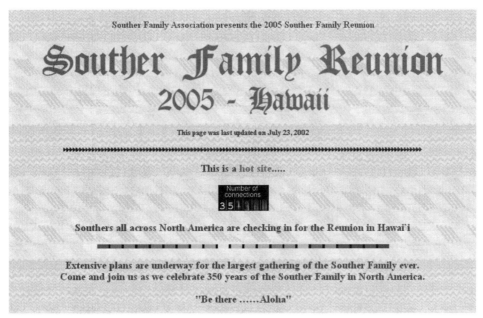

Figure 3.1 Advance promotion for the Souther Family Reunion

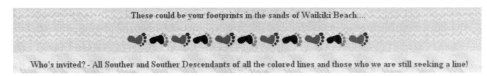

Figure 3.2 A warm invitation to walk Waikiki Beach

Is there an "old family homestead" or historic spot connected to your family's past? "Going home" is a big draw for reunions, especially for those family groups who long ago moved to another part of the country. If their children have never seen the lands of their ancestors, a reunion can be a great incentive to make the trip.

Is there convenient transportation? Since family members have likely scattered to all parts of the country (and perhaps the world), they will probably base their decision whether to attend on the accessibility of the location. Flying is most complex, in terms of price and ease in making connections. Choosing a city that is a hub or that offers the most direct flights makes the idea of flying in for a reunion more palatable. And don't locate the actual reunion too far from the airport—requiring car miles after air miles may be too much to ask of elderly relatives and families with young children.

Will it be easy to find for drivers? It will be important to include a good map of the selected reunion location in later mailings. Chapter 10 offers some good suggestions, such as making signs near the site to help travelers find their way.

Are there volunteers who can pick up attendees from the airport? If the nearest airport is within twenty-five miles from the reunion site, perhaps volunteers can pick up the traveling cousins. If the airport is farther away, be sure to distribute bus schedules and information about rental cars in later mailings.

Are there affordable lodging options? If your reunion is held in a setting that does not include sleeping rooms, you should find rooms for those traveling a distance. A variety of options in various price ranges will help people select appropriate housing that fits into their budget. Chapter 8 discusses lodging options in more detail.

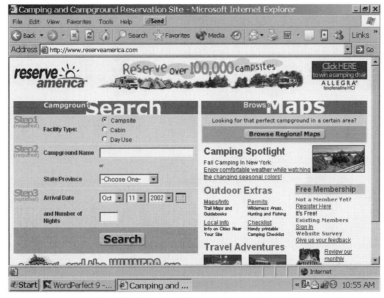

Figure 3.3 One hundred thousand campsites online at Reserve America

Is the reunion site accessible for those with limited mobility? Most public hotels and motels are required to comply with the requirements of the Americans with Disabilities Act (ADA) by providing accessible accommodations or publicizing access limitations. But to make certain that Uncle Paul will be able to find a place that will accommodate his wheelchair, be sure to confirm which recommended places are suitable for those with special needs. Online reservation sites, such as *www.reserveamerica.com* (see Figure 3.3), provide specific information about available special accommodations at campsites.

National and State Parks

America's large network of national and state parks offers great locations and a wide variety of enjoyable activities for a reunion group. Most have picnic and camping facilities, as well as such options as boating, swimming, hiking trails, beaches, and athletic fields. The National Park Service maintains an online reservation center with details and deadlines for scenic spots across the United States, including national parks, campgrounds, and tours of historic sites. (Some of their popular sites, such as Yosemite National Park, accept reservations only five months in advance, which works against a plan being made a year or two before a desired date.) Visit *reservations.nps.gov/parklist.cfm* for more information.

Many states also offer great places for reunions. Through the State of Texas Web site *(www.tpwd.state.tx.us/park/admin/res)*, you can make reservations at state parks

"Celebrate 100 Years for 100 Days" was California's slogan for the hundredth anniversary of Big Basin Redwoods State Park in 2002. They offered one hundred days of dance, music, theater, lectures, and special events.

and historic sites. It's easy to search online for such services in other states: Enter the state name plus the words *"park reservation"* in a search engine such as Google *(www.google.com)*—you'll see lots of opportunities to research. Appendix A lists online resources for the fifty state parks systems.

City, Suburbs, Countryside?

Locations in a downtown urban area are usually more expensive than those in suburban or rural areas. In addition to cost, however, your choice of place depends on the type of activities you want to engage in. Many cities have tourism agencies or Convention and Visitors Bureaus, and they welcome inquiries from reunion groups. Figure 3.4 shows that Birmingham, Alabama, would love to host your family reunion.

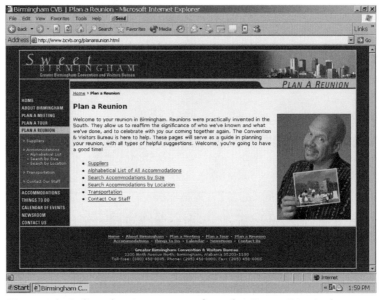

Figure 3.4 Online planning resources from the Greater Birmingham Convention & Visitors Bureau

If you expect a large crowd, these agencies can also provide maps and guides to attractions and lodging, and they can work with you to negotiate packages to suit your needs. To enhance your success with prompt and comprehensive services, contact such agencies early in your planning process.

The National Trust for Historic Preservation publishes an annual list called a "Dozen Distinctive Destinations," sites selected as "exciting alternatives to more homogenized vacation spots." The list for 2002 included Asheville, North Carolina; Butte, Montana; Fernandina Beach, Florida; Ferndale, California; Frederick, Maryland; Holland, Michigan; Milan, Ohio; Morristown, New Jersey; Saratoga Springs, New York; Silver City, New Mexico; Walla Walla, Washington; and Westerly, Rhode Island. Find more information online at *www.nthp.org/dozen_distinctive_destinations.*

Sights and Sites

Once you select the location—state, county, community—you'll need to choose a specific facility. Consider three key factors:

- Space
- Price
- Features

The Right Space

Your preliminary family survey, described in Chapter 1, helps determine the projected size of your reunion crowd, which then helps you narrow down the choices for a facility or location in terms of space needed. The ages of the participants are another factor to consider. If you expect many young children to attend or several seniors with mobility challenges, don't select a boat trip to a remote island campground. Children need safe supervised spaces in which to frolic, and seniors will welcome comfortable seating with rest rooms close by.

The Right Price

Cost is a significant item and must be considered as you select your reunion site. The total cost includes more than the rental fees for a facility. You also have to consider charges for transportation to and from the site, food, parking fees, and entrance fees. More of these considerations are discussed in Chapter 4.

The Right Features

Besides the actual reunion site, what other "sights" or attractions does the proposed location provide? Perhaps there's a swimming pool or lake nearby that permits boating or fishing. Maybe a miniature golf course could be included as an activity. What theaters, museums, shopping centers, amusement parks, sports facilities, or other points of interest are nearby? Such opportunities are attractive additions to your reunion publicity materials—especially for those families who have not visited the area before.

Onsite Visits

Whether you are considering a picnic pavilion in the park, a cache of condos at the beach, or a castle in Spain or Scotland, it's best to have someone inspect the actual location. That person may be the producer or a trusted family member who lives in

Wood Work

For the second Wood Family Reunion in July 1999, I sought location advice from relatives living near Lebanon, New Hampshire. The cousin who generously donated the country club spot in 1994 had moved to Florida and discontinued his club membership, though he was one of the most active committee members seeking a new site.

After considering several places, we selected a ski lodge. Off season in July, it was available for rental to groups for a modest fee. I lived five hundred miles away, but the local cousins checked out the prices, space, and features. I had one opportunity on a business trip to Boston to make a quick drive there and check it out for myself—perfect! The site included a large open room indoors, tables and chairs, outside decks, ample lawns, a large parking lot, and a beautiful mountain in the backyard.

the area, but it's important that a written report from your onsite inspector be distributed to the reunion planning team. If several different people review a number of potential locations, send them a common checklist so their responses can be easily compared. Figures 3.5 and 3.6 are two checklists—one for facilities such as parks, community halls, and rental properties, and the other for a hotel or conference center. Add any items that are important to you. When the planning team for your reunion selects a facility and the business manager negotiates specific contracts, the checklists will help guide them in those processes.

For international locations, look to ratings found in travel publications or on the Internet and ask friends and acquaintances who have personal experiences with certain locations. Some travel professionals specialize in arranging tours for family groups to ancestral homelands. At *www.cyndislist.com/travel.htm,* you will find many references to travel resources.

Checklist for Evaluating Facilities Other Than Hotels or Restaurants

☐ Have other family reunions been held here? If so, ask for references and contact them.

☐ What are the "peak seasons" and "off seasons" for rates?

☐ What is the parking situation? Any fees? Policy on pets?

☐ Is there a variety of lodging options in the area?

☐ Where is the nearest RV campground?

☐ Where is the nearest airport?   Train station? Bus depot? Interstate highway?

☐ What services are included in a rental?

☐ Where is the nearest rental service to acquire other equipment or supplies?

☐ What are the policies regarding serving food? Alcoholic beverages?

☐ _____

☐ _____

Figure 3.5 Checklist for evaluating facilities other than hotels or restaurants

---

Checklist for Evaluating Hotels, Conference Centers, and Resorts

- ☐ Have other family reunions been held here? If so, ask for references and contact them.
- ☐ What are the "peak seasons" and "off seasons" for rates?
- ☐ What is the parking situation? Any fees?
- ☐ How many sleeping rooms are available?
- ☐ Are meeting rooms included? Or at an extra cost? If so, what is the cost and what does it cover? Are there tables for displays? Audio-visual equipment?
- ☐ Are there meal options? Is special group seating available? Is there beverage service in the meeting room?
- ☐ Are there recreational facilities? A pool?   Fitness room? What are the hours of operation?
- ☐ _____
- ☐ _____

Figure 3.6 Checklist for evaluating hotels, conference centers, and resorts

The International Gathering of the Clan MacLean took place in 2002 on the Isle of Mull in Scotland. More than a year prior, I made reservations for lodging at a bed-and-breakfast inn that had a wonderful Web site with photographs, prices, menus, and an e-mail address for the innkeepers.

Using a timetable for your reunion planning is the best way to chart your path toward success. Of course, your plans will be modified and changed several times during the course of production, as you make different decisions along the way. In Figure 3.7, Production Timetable 3 shows where you should be at this stage of production, as we build on the steps taken earlier. Now that you have a plan, people to help, and a place for the reunion, the next order of production planning involves the finances—the dollars and sense.

Production Timetable 3
12 to 24 months prior:

☑ Decide to hold a family reunion.
☑ Survey the audience—the family.
☑ Begin to develop a mailing list.
☑ Consider the time, place, location, and theme.
☑ Hold auditions for the cast and crew.
☑ Select the producer and the business manager.
☐ Survey the proposed places and locations.
☐ Select the time, place, location, and theme.

Figure 3.7 Production Timetable 3

Box Office Prices: Dollars and Sense

Money Talks: What Does It Say?

"HOW MUCH MONEY DO WE NEED?" AND "HOW ARE WE GOING TO GET it?" "Do we want to just break even or to make money for the next reunion?" These are key questions for your team. During your first few planning sessions, you need to come to a consensus on the financial goals of your event. Usually, as the project begins, planning team members have some out-of-pocket expenses for mailing and phone calls. Ask them to keep track of what they spend. Even if some generous family members donate part of the costs, be sure to record all those amounts so you have a total picture of the finances for your reports—that way, people who need to be reimbursed can be. Requesting a deposit several months in advance for a reservation is a good way to bring in early income to help defray start-up expenses.

Breaking Even

For a first reunion, it's reasonable to plan that income will match expenses. Keep in mind that some expenses are fixed, while others are optional. Typical of fixed expenses are leasing a space, hiring a photographer, and hiring or providing entertainment. Once you sign a contract or make a deposit, that expense remains the same regardless of the final number of attendees. The remaining costs need to be researched and allocated carefully so that money brought in through ticket prices covers all costs.

Making Money

If you want to end up with a "profit" at the end of your reunion, of course you must raise more dollars than you spend. Some families who hold regular reunions decide to build up a treasury with various fund-raising efforts (as described in Chapter 15). Other sources of income, such as raffles or auctions, cannot be predicted with much accuracy for a first reunion; they are discussed later in this chapter.

Banking

Almost from the moment you decide to hold a family reunion, money—particularly, where to bank it—becomes an issue. Look for a bank that offers basic services with as few fees as possible. Consider having two signatures on file for the checking account so that someone is always available to access funds when needed.

As an alternative to a separate bank account, find out whether a family member belongs to a credit union. Or arrange for a sub-account to be kept in a trusted individual's personal or business account. Do this only with the clear understanding that regular reports must be issued before and after the event.

Sources of Income

Registration Fees

Setting the price of a reunion registration depends, of course, on how much of the expenses must be covered by that fee. In addition to food and beverage costs, you have the costs of facility rental, equipment rental, printing and postage, and other items presented later in this chapter. To set the registration fee, aim to divide the projected costs by the anticipated number of participants.

Age Categories for Registration Fees

At my family reunions, we used these guidelines for ticket prices:

- Ages 12 and over: full adult charge
- Ages 6 to 11: half adult charge
- Ages 5 and under: no charge

Most reunions scale registration fees for different members of family groups (under ten years old, over sixty-five, and so on). Categorizing payment according to age helps provide a reasonable rate for family groups.

Donations

Donations are a great way to add income *and* reduce reunion expenses. They can be in the form of money or in-kind contributions, and they can come from reunion participants or outside sources. Does Uncle Dave work in a food market? If so, can he obtain discounts for food and supplies? How about Cousin Ned who works in a print shop? Perhaps he can obtain a donation in the form of free printing of fliers and other mailings. Pair occupations and workplaces of attendees with related merchandise or services they could provide at a deep discount, or even free.

When the facility and food were donated for my first Wood family reunion, many first reunion problems were instantly solved. Those donations, combined with other family contributions after all expenses were paid, meant we had money left over. We then donated the remainder in the family's name to the local historical society, which had helped so much with our research.

Since many businesses, large and small, provide giveaways as part of their advertising budgets, use family members who live in the community to approach local merchants or the Convention and Visitors Bureau for direct donations of items, discounts on purchases, or a combination of both. (Figure 4.1 shows a sample letter soliciting donations.) You can create "goodie" bags to hold the souvenirs, coupons for restaurants, and merchandise discounts.

There are many smaller ways in which nonmonetary donations can reduce reunion expenses. The easiest method is to announce in reunion mailings and newsletters, with specific examples, what kinds of donations of goods and services would be welcomed. "Advertise" for experienced volunteer videographers and DJs; ask if any family members are employed in local schools and suggest they try to get a loan of sports equipment.

Seed Money

Broadway shows are financed by a group of investors called "backers" who provide the start-up money to develop a new production. Advance ticket sales add to the available funds and indicate the public's early interest. Perhaps you can ask a small group of supportive family members to make an early deposit toward reunion expenses.

While backers on Broadway invest money with hopes of future returns from a profitable and successful production, your team will be making a direct contribution to the event. After carefully recording the donors and amounts of donations, place the

The Marshall Family Association
Descendants of John and Elizabeth (Parker) Marshall

Pioneer Settlers of
Ourtown 1878

January 5, 2004

James A. Miller
Ourtown Department Store
1000 Main Street
Ourtown, USA 12345-6789

Dear Mr. Miller,

On July 15, at South Park Pavilion in Ourtown, we expect about one hundred descendants of one of our town's earliest pioneer families, John and Elizabeth (Parker) Marshall, to come together from many states to celebrate their heritage and to honor their ancestors.

A special project is planned to restore the old family cemetery located on the Back Road, which has fallen into disrepair. The fund-raising for this worthwhile community project will begin at this Marshall Family Reunion.

We would appreciate merchandise and/or service donations that we can offer as raffle items for our event. Your gift will be acknowledged at our event and in all our publicity.

Jeffrey Marshall, of our Reunion Committee, will call on you the week of January 20 to discuss how your kind and generous donation will bring you the benefit of community goodwill.

Thank you for your consideration. We look forward to your support.

Sincerely,

Your name
Your address
Your phone number

Figure 4.1 Sample letter to solicit donations

money in the reunion's bank account and let it grow until you need it. At the end of the event, there may be a small surplus that can serve as seed money for the next one.

Raffles

Raffles are another way to help meet reunion expenses. All income raised this way should be recorded in your financial reports. If someone wants to donate an expensive item to be raffled, be sure to check with a tax adviser about any tax benefits that might go to the donor. Give the donor a receipt, and keep records of the number of tickets sold. You'll find ideas for special raffle items in Chapter 11.

Sale of Merchandise

When you go to a Broadway show, the ticket price is just the entry fee. You find the lobby filled with tables of souvenirs and mementos of the occasion that the management hopes you will decide you simply must buy. Sales tables are common at many reunions, but be aware that the profit margin can vary widely. T-shirts or coffee cups emblazoned with a reunion logo, as items to be included in the registration fee or to be sold separately, will not produce a major profit. Merchants know that they must price an item at least double the wholesale cost in order to make a profit. Since small orders for personalized items can be expensive, you don't want to double that cost for purchasers. (More about items for sale in Ye Olde Reunion Shoppe can be found in Chapter 11.)

Future sales of reunion videos or family cookbooks or calendars, on the other hand, can provide considerable income to the reunion treasury. Other popular reunion items that sell well are baseball caps, painters' hats, tote bags, coffee mugs, pens or pencils, frisbees, key rings, sweatshirts, note pads, even stuffed animals with the family name. You name it, and someone will put your name on it. For one of my reunions, I considered all kinds of unique items but settled on a simple choice and ordered a bunch of ballpoint pens that read "Wood Family of Lebanon, NH, since 1766."

> **Allow plenty of time for delivery of imprinted items. Add them to the timetable months ahead of the reunion.**

Bake Sale

A bake sale works well for a one-day event held near where many of the participants live—it isn't easy or safe to tote fresh apple pies on an airplane or in a car trunk for several hundred miles. Part of your planning should include determining whether the facility you use permits bake sales. While a state park will, it is likely a hotel will say no. If you're meeting at an outdoor location, consider the weather and plan for supplies to cover and protect the items from the direct sun or sudden showers. Since frosted items like cakes and cupcakes may not fare well in the sunshine, consider breads, rolls, pies, cookies, and other less perishable items. Assign a team to receive, display, and sell the items. And make sure they keep records of the items sold and the money received.

Family Flea Markets

Everyone loves a good bargain, and we all know that one man's trash is another man's treasure. A flea market is a very popular event—when most attendees are local and can provide goods for resale. Get donations by "advertising" in newsletters and other pre-reunion communications; include a full description of the kinds of items desired for donation. No broken TVs or litters of kittens! Create a special team to receive, price, tag, and display the items, as well as cashiers who keep a written record of the income for each item. For tax purposes, some family members will ask for a receipt for the donation, so have a receipt book handy.

Family Auction

A family auction based on early donations provides lots of entertainment as families compete to bid for items. Many families report this is the most fun of the day. Think about some "specials" to add to the excitement. Can a gifted craftsperson create a family quilt or afghan? Is a family artist willing to contribute a painting, sculpture, or professionally framed photograph? Will a local restaurant donate a free dinner? Is there one outgoing family member who would make the perfect auctioneer?

Managing Sales Events

Newsletters and announcements can both publicize the details of the special sales tables, flea market, or auction and encourage contributions. Each of these sales or events should be delegated to a separate team to arrange for donations, display, and staffing during the reunion. After any expenses for display tables or signs, all the receipts will be profit and can add welcome funds to the reunion treasury. Detailed record keeping is a must, and the business manager will instruct the various teams on how to handle and report receipts of cash and checks.

We have a silent auction on the last night of the Hytrek Reunion to help finance the next one. One aunt is a master gardener and brings fresh produce, which fetches a good price. A cousin made a family tree quilt; it might be amateurish by some standards, but this one-of-a-kind handmade item sold for $150.

—Bobbi King

Typical Expenses

While details of particular expenses are covered throughout the book, this is an overview of typical expenses. You and your team will develop and determine the exact categories that apply to your reunion, once you decide on the what-where-when specifics that best meet the needs and wishes of your own family. Remember that all expenses need not have equal cash income to balance the budget, as there are ways to offset many expenses with donations of time, talents, merchandise, and services.

Facility Rental and Permit Fees

Beyond the basic facility rental fee, there are almost always taxes and gratuities to add to the bottom line. Keep in mind that many facilities require an early deposit.

Parks, campgrounds, and other public facilities often have permit fees for use, with guidelines and regulations that apply to your function. Read the details of every written agreement to make sure that any regulations are acceptable to your group. If alcohol is not permitted on the premises, you must notify everyone about it lest Cousin Jack tote in a cooler filled with beer.

Food and Refreshments

The actual costs of food and refreshments vary considerably, depending on whether you hire a caterer, have different families bring items for a potluck meal, or purchase food supplies to be prepared by a food team offsite or onsite. Once you decide how to feed everyone, you can develop a food budget. Even with a caterer, you probably want other refreshments available at registration and during activities. Consider the weather as you determine how many cold drinks and container tubs, and how much ice you need. Price it all out ahead of time. Ask merchants to help develop guidelines about how much you need for the number of people you expect.

Professional Photographers and Entertainers

A group photo of the reunion provides a popular souvenir of the occasion, as well as a memento for the next reunion and future generations. For budget purposes, get estimates from professionals. Do you want a professional just for the group shot? Can family members fill in with other videos and candid shots? You'll see in the sample budget later in this chapter that at one family reunion, we hired a professional photographer for one hour. He charged one hundred dollars and then reduced that fee according to the number of copies ordered that day from family members.

It's more fun to use family members as entertainers, volunteer DJs, and musicians, if you can find the talent that sometimes hides in large family groups. But if you do hire professionals, check references carefully and see or hear samples of their work. Good photographers will have portfolios, and entertainers have promotional tapes or videos.

Decorations

You may find that your reunion site needs a little or lots of decoration. Prices for decorations vary, according to how elaborate a décor you choose and who supplies it. You may be eating at picnic tables overlooking a lake for which nature has provided spectacular "decoration," or you may have a hotel banquet room with streamers and table centerpieces.

Printing

Throughout the planning and right up to the day of the reunion, there will be fliers, newsletters, programs, award certificates, name badges, and other printing tasks for the reunion. Some jobs may be done on a computer; others will need to be taken to a copy shop. Most discount office supply stores offer the best value for reams of paper and large boxes of envelopes. Estimate the cost of these supplies and service charges for the budget.

Postage and Phone Calls

The number of mailings and their weight multiplied by the number of recipients determines the postage costs. Three or four mailings are typical, though the number of recipients will change. A policy on long-distance phone calls needs to be established early in the process and communicated to all who will be making calls on behalf of the reunion. The sample voucher form in Figure 4.2 can be used to reimburse expenses like phone calls and supplies.

Equipment Rental

Will you need to rent tables, chairs, a tent, or audio-visual equipment? If so, get estimates in advance to add to the budget. Also seek other ways to obtain them. Is someone in the family able to borrow equipment from a club, organization, or facility? Can local families tote along extra folding yard furniture?

Prizes and Awards

Chapters 9 and 11 discuss the need for many prizes, especially for children. The costs of these awards can vary. Ribbons with cards on the back to personalize for the winner can cost two dollars each, or you can make them from supplies at a fabric store. Award certificates can be printed on a computer or purchased as fancy framed items. My sample budget lumped together contest prizes, door prizes, and raffle prizes into one category.

Equipment and Supplies for Games and Activities

I have been able to beg or borrow all the athletic equipment needed for my family reunions. If you use some of the suggestions in Chapter 9 for arts and crafts projects, you may need to buy some supplies. If you hold a putting contest, you will need a few balls, which probably can be gathered from the discards in family members' golfing bags—or donated by the local golf course. Badminton and croquet sets are usually hiding out in some relative's basement or garage. Though the actual costs for these items should be low, you should budget an amount.

Our Family Reunion
Expense Voucher Form

Please complete this form, and attach all receipts and other documentation.

Name:_____ Committee:_____

Address:_____ Phone:_____

Purpose of Expense   Amount of Expense

1._____ $_____

2._____ $_____

3._____ $_____

4._____ $_____

5._____ $_____

                              Total: $_____

              Less Cash Advance Received: $_____

                 Actual Reimbursement: $_____

Signature:_____ Date:_____

Approved by Committee Chairperson

_____ Date:_____
    Signature

Approved by Treasurer

_____ Date:_____
    Signature

Check#_____ Paid on:_____

Budget Category _____

Figure 4.2 Sample voucher form

Contracts

Most family reunions involve at least one contract requiring negotiation and signature. The likely candidates are the hall, hotel, park pavilion, or other facility; the catering service; professional musicians and photographers; and supply-rental companies. Either the producer or the business manager should assume contractual responsibilities. As with any contract, it is wise to read all the small print and be sure that the terms cover exactly what you negotiated and agreed to. If you are contracting to rent equipment, visit the supplier and be specific about the grade and type of item you want. Make sure the exact model numbers and items, as well as delivery dates and pick-up dates, appear in the contract.

I was on the committee for a weekend hotel event for three hundred people at which we wanted coffee service available all day and evening. The contract didn't specify the price, and we were shocked to be billed nearly forty dollars a gallon for a large quantity we couldn't prove was actually served—an oversight that nearly broke our budget.

Budget and Banking

Set Event Costs and Budget

The business manager develops a working budget based on the selected location, facility, and type of event. The planning team—producer, stage manager, and other key persons—then discusses the numbers and agrees on the ticket prices.

What should the ticket price cover? Will it be one fee for the whole production? Or will you charge extra for optional events, like narrated city tours, visits to ancestral properties, or a golf tournament? It's hard to set the price until you have a firm grip on the number of people attending and the different price categories. Once you agree to a per-person price with your suppliers, you are stuck with it—so detailed planning is essential.

Preliminary Budget for One-Day Family Reunion
Based on 100 persons (75 adults, 25 children)

Expense Item	Description	Cost
Facility rental	Park pavilion	500.
Meal	Catered	1200.
Snacks, beverages		100.
Printing	40 memory books, programs, signs	200.
Mailings	3 mailings to 40	120.
Awards, prizes	50 ribbons, flag, etc.	150.
Photographer	1 hour Saturday	100.
Reunion Shoppe	50 T-shirts @ $6	300.
Miscellaneous	Contingency	270.
	Estimated Costs Total	**$2,940.**

Income Source	Details	Amount
Registration	75 adults @ $20 25 children @ $10	1500. 250.
Raffle tickets	200 @ $2	400.
Reunion Shoppe	50 T-shirts @ $8 Donated items	400. 200.
Family auction	30 items donated	500.
	Estimated Income Total	**$3,250.**

Figure 4.3 Sample preliminary budget

Preliminary Budget Estimates

It is smart to be conservative and to slightly overestimate expenditures in the planning stages, since final costs may well be 10 percent higher than your best estimates—especially since you could be planning a year in advance. Figure 4.3 provides a sample budget that covers most of the basics—and is easily adaptable to your family's needs.

Incentives for Early Registration

Once your fees have been established and you have announced the fee structure through publicity, newsletters, and mailings, consider asking for early reservations or deposits. Early payment not only provides needed cash for the treasury, but it also demonstrates a commitment to attend because people who pay in advance are more likely to show up. You will also have a tentative count of participants, which will help in planning for food and facilities.

To encourage early registration, consider a discounted ticket price before a certain deadline or an extra "gift" awarded at the event for those early registrants. At past reunions, we've given a simple prize ribbon called "Early Bird," as well as seconds on dessert.

Refund Policy

Any family can have last-minute emergencies that prevent travel plans—perhaps a reservation for six persons changes to four when someone becomes ill or two teenagers opt out. Early on in the planning process, you need to decide on a refund policy and make sure it is clearly communicated in all your reunion materials. Many reunions establish a refund policy based on time of notification, with a cancellation fee of ten dollars for notices received up to one week before the event. Last-minute cancellations can be considered on an individual basis and refunds made after the reunion. Just remember, if you give a guaranteed number to a facility or caterer, at a certain point you are liable for those costs.

Reimbursing Personal Expenses

You also need to develop a policy and procedure for reimbursing personal expenses. This primarily entails the submission of receipts with a voucher before reimbursement. It may not always be possible or prudent to wait for the business manager/treasurer to prepare a check before buying some supplies, and some team members may find it easier and more convenient—often to take advantage of sale prices—to purchase items with their own cash, checks, or credit cards. This is all fine, as long as the proper paper trail is followed. A sample voucher form was shown in Figure 4.2.

Act 1 and its four chapters have given you the production design information and backstage basics for planning and organizing your family reunion. In Act 2, you'll find seven chapters with a detailed script for turning this preliminary planning into a polished performance.

Act 2
Backstage Preparations

CHAPTER 5

The Script: Record Keeping

FEW SUCCESSFUL PRODUCTIONS ARE IMPROMPTU IMPROVISATIONS. Scripts and records are developed, revised, and updated, and serve to keep the crew and cast informed about the event. One of the first things you should develop is a record-keeping system. It helps your team stay focused, and it provides a history of the planning and production process to pass on to future production teams.

Paperwork Priorities

What do you need to know and record? Obviously, the date and location selected for the reunion. The names and numbers of all those who have volunteered or been recruited to work on reunion teams should also be at your fingertips. As your team establishes specific tasks and priorities, you'll need to be able to track their status on a given day. Scribbling notes on the back of an envelope works for a list to take to the supermarket, but for a major function, it will create only more piles of old envelopes.

Chapter 4 presented details about the financial records generated for a reunion. You want to make sure the business manager is tracking income and expenses and producing reports when you need them. How often depends on your schedule and scope—in the early stages, monthly is sufficient. But as the date draws near, keep closer tabs on the budget to make sure everything you have planned can be paid for.

Keeping track of the potential audience for your production means regular revisions to a list that includes name, address, contact numbers (phone, fax, e-mail), plus names

Once upon a time, all information and experience was stored in the minds and memories of the elders and the storytellers, who passed it on to others in the village. Then writing was invented, first in pictures and then with various alphabets. This was the beginning of what we now call "information management."

and ages of all family members in that household. As you prepare each round of mailings, note which families were sent a package. Since the list will likely expand as you locate more and more extended family groups, a tracking system becomes essential.

A second layer of record tracking concerns preregistrations. Who's coming? How many in different age categories? Did they send back personal information for the family history book? Did they pay a deposit? How much? What's the balance due?

Simple Systems

My grandmother left a small notebook in which she listed a few reunions in the early part of the twentieth century and the names of those who attended. As you see in

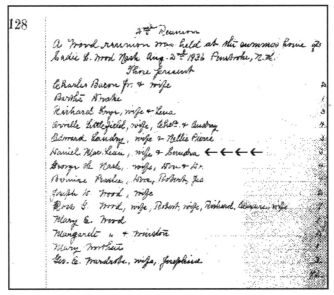

Figure 5.1 Record of 1936 Wood Reunion attendance

Figure 5.1, I even found my own name on the 1936 list—I was six months old at my very first reunion! At our reunions, we enjoy looking at these lists from the 1930s and 1940s and finding our family members' names, even though most of us cannot personally recall the events we attended as small children. Of course, it is still possible to keep the records of a reunion handwritten on file cards or in notebooks, but it isn't very practical today when so many better systems are available.

For Small Reunions

If you plan a small gathering of family members and you know where each of them lives today, your record keeping can be minimal. Recently, our family held a week-long "minireunion" at the beach. Like many families, our children are grown and scattered across the country. There are now over thirty of us, including children, step-children, spouses, partners, and grandchildren. My sister organized the event; she rented two large adjacent beachfront houses a year in advance so that the dates could be set on everyone's calendar.

Her record keeping consisted of dividing the total initial deposit costs by the numbers in each participating family group, keeping all informed of details by telephone and e-mail, and recording the current status on a few sheets of paper. Each family paid a portion of the rental based on how many beds and rooms they occupied, meaning couples without children paid less than those with children. During the week together, we saved the receipts for food and other group supplies purchased by any of the participants for a final financial assessment and report. The details were informal. When folks returned from a deep-sea fishing excursion with many pounds of fresh tuna for dinner, we counted that as a donation.

For a larger group gathering, the simplest system is to get a portable file container from the office supply store—such as the sturdy plastic ones with a lip that holds hanging files. There you can keep all your paper records and receipts in file folders, labeled alphabetically by surname, date, or topic. Color coding can help distinguish one group of records from another.

Technology's Tools

From the time the U.S. federal census was instituted in 1790 until the 1880s, the census takers wrote their entries in log books, then made copies to send to governmental agencies. Each time a copy was made, human error crept in. When tabulations of results were made, another series of errors popped up and the summaries were often suspect. Not until the 1880s, when an enterprising young man named Herman Hollerith invented a punch card system of recording information, did the census begin to achieve its goals of counting the people to determine representation in Congress. After he retired in 1921, Hollerith sold his tabulating business. In 1924, it was renamed International Business Machines—IBM—and a new era in information management was born.

All record keeping for the 1994 and 1999 Wood family reunions was done on computer. Each time I've upgraded computers since then, I've transferred all the old files to the new machines, so I have a historical record of them. Figures 5.2, 5.3, and 5.4 show you examples of forms I developed for a database I created to track an early reunion. First is a data form sent out to gather personal information for the family history database, followed by a form to collect registration information. At the bottom of the personal data form is a box for the record keeper to note the date the information was received and the date it was entered into the database. That provided a cross-check for me when a lot of forms came in all at once.

Spreadsheet and Database Programs

Spreadsheet and database programs are powerful aids in organizing and retrieving information. The most popular ones today are Microsoft Excel and Corel Quattro Pro, spreadsheet programs that let you organize your data into lists and then summarize, compare, and present your data graphically. Microsoft Access and Corel Paradox are relational database programs that allow you to access, link, and manipulate the information contained in multiple related databases. These programs can handle millions of items and can be shared by more than one user at a time. Experienced users can create a spreadsheet or database for the reunion event. If you have a computer-savvy person on your team, this is an option for your record-keeping tasks.

Specialized Financial Software Programs

As reunion finances become more complex, you'll want your business manager to work with software programs for budgeting finances. Two popular programs mentioned earlier are Quicken and Microsoft Money, which allow you to list and track all categories of income and expenses and produce graphs and reports to share with others. Figure 5.5 shows a sample printout from a financial report produced five months before the 1999 reunion.

Data Sheet for Wood Family History (My Generation)

Describe your own family group. If you are not sure, enter data with a "?" to provide clues for further research.

My full name at birth		Nickname:
My birth date/place		
My Father's full name		
His birth date/place		
His death date/place		
My Mother's maiden name		
Her birth date/place		
Her death date/place		
Their marriage date/place		
My Brothers' and Sisters' names, birth dates/places Please give current names and addresses for all living siblings on back of sheet.		
I married		
Marriage date/place		
Spouse birth date/place		
Spouse's Father		
Spouse's Mother		
Full name at birth of all of my Children from all marriages, with birth dates/places Please give addresses for all grown children living elsewhere on back of sheet.		
Prior marriages of mine (dates/names)		
My present occupation		
My present address/ phone/fax/e-mail		

Write any other information you choose on the back of this page.

Please return to: *[my name, address, phone, fax, and e-mail address]*

Date received:	Entered in database:	Other:

Figure 5.2 Data sheet for personal information

Reservation Form for 1999 Wood Family Reunion

Name:	
Address:	
Phone:	E-mail:

(Feel free to copy this form and send it to others we may not have on the list.)

☐ Sorry, I can't attend the Wood Family Reunion, but I am interested in remaining on the mailing list and sharing in the data exchange.

☐ Yes! We're coming to the Wood Family Reunion. Count in the following for the luncheon.

Name (for name tag)	Age (if child 12 & under)	Relationship to me	$22. Adult 12 & over $12. Child 5–11 Free for kids 4 & under
Self:			$
Others:			$
			$
			$
			$
			$
			$
			$
		TOTAL	

Please return to: *[my name and address]*

(If your group is larger than 10, copy this sheet and send both back. **See other side also.**)

To date, deposit received from you is $_____

Deposit/Balance—check enclosed with this reservation: $_____
(You can pay at the event, but advance payment is appreciated as we must pay the final caterer bill a week before the event.)

Figure 5.3 Reservation form, front

Optional Events:

Yes No

☐ ☐ **Friday:**   Informal evening gathering, especially for out-of-towners, but all are welcome! Exact details will be sent to you—likely a meal together at a local family-type restaurant near Lebanon.

☐ ☐ **Sunday:**   8:30 A.M.—Dutch-Treat Breakfast Buffet at Radisson Hotel in West Lebanon

☐ ☐   10:30 A.M.—DAR Grave-Marking Ceremony for Joseph Wood at the Pine Tree Cemetery

☐ ☐   (Followed by)
Informal Tour of Wood Farms

We're invited to Wood Farms in Kirby, Vermont—four lovely farms within a mile, occupied by descendants of the Luther Wood family since 1816. One of them, appropriately called Kinship Farm, has a large dairy operation of interest to children of all ages.

There are also former Wood properties around Lebanon that we can visit. Some of these were on the tour in 1994, but many new participants may be joining this year.

If touring with us, please indicate your preference:

☐ Want to see the Vermont dairy farms (11:30 A.M.–3:30 P.M.). (We'll work out some lunch arrangements for this tour.)

☐ Will join for a Lebanon area tour only (11:30 A.M.–1:00 P.M.).

We'll try to arrange for both tours, but as they'll happen at the same time, please sign up for only one.

If you have any questions about lodging, directions, or reservations, please contact Sandy anytime: *[my home phone and e-mail address]*.

Figure 5.4 Reservation form, back

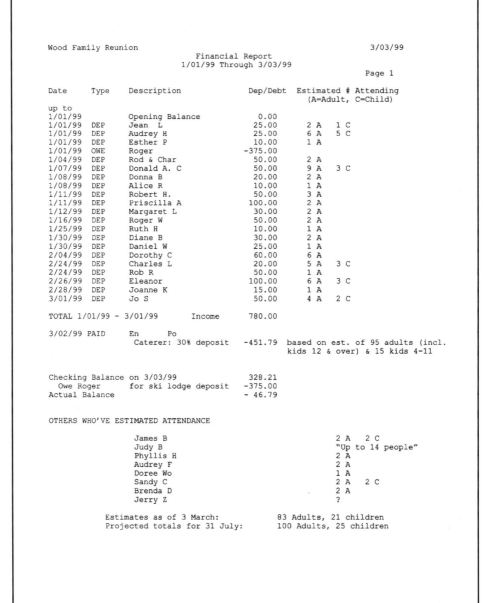

```
Wood Family Reunion                                      3/03/99
                            Financial Report
                        1/01/99 Through 3/03/99
                                                        Page 1

Date      Type    Description          Dep/Debt  Estimated # Attending
                                                 (A=Adult, C=Child)
up to
1/01/99           Opening Balance         0.00
1/01/99   DEP     Jean  L                25.00    2 A   1 C
1/01/99   DEP     Audrey H               25.00    6 A   5 C
1/01/99   DEP     Esther P               10.00    1 A
1/01/99   OWE     Roger                -375.00
1/04/99   DEP     Rod & Char             50.00    2 A
1/07/99   DEP     Donald A. C            50.00    9 A   3 C
1/08/99   DEP     Donna B                20.00    2 A
1/08/99   DEP     Alice R                10.00    1 A
1/11/99   DEP     Robert H.              50.00    3 A
1/11/99   DEP     Priscilla A           100.00    2 A
1/12/99   DEP     Margaret L             30.00    2 A
1/16/99   DEP     Roger W                50.00    2 A
1/25/99   DEP     Ruth H                 10.00    1 A
1/30/99   DEP     Diane B                30.00    2 A
1/30/99   DEP     Daniel W               25.00    1 A
2/04/99   DEP     Dorothy C              60.00    6 A
2/24/99   DEP     Charles L              20.00    5 A   3 C
2/24/99   DEP     Rob R                  50.00    1 A
2/26/99   DEP     Eleanor               100.00    6 A   3 C
2/28/99   DEP     Joanne K               15.00    1 A
3/01/99   DEP     Jo S                   50.00    4 A   2 C

TOTAL 1/01/99 - 3/01/99      Income      780.00

3/02/99 PAID      En      Po
                  Caterer: 30% deposit -451.79  based on est. of 95 adults (incl.
                                                kids 12 & over) & 15 kids 4-11


Checking Balance on 3/03/99              328.21
  Owe Roger     for ski lodge deposit  -375.00
Actual Balance                         - 46.79


OTHERS WHO'VE ESTIMATED ATTENDANCE

              James B                          2 A    2 C
              Judy B                           "Up to 14 people"
              Phyllis H                        2 A
              Audrey F                         2 A
              Doree Wo                         1 A
              Sandy C                          2 A    2 C
              Brenda D                         2 A
              Jerry Z                          ?

         Estimates as of 3 March:        83 Adults, 21 children
         Projected totals for 31 July:  100 Adults, 25 children
```

Figure 5.5 First financial report, five months before reunion

Specialized Reunion Software Programs

Software programs that specialize in reunion planning have been developed in recent years; they vary in features and costs. Some have integrated database and financial capabilities that replace the need for separate spreadsheet, database, or financial software programs. These new software programs make reunion planning much easier, offering the following capabilities:

- Address book and mailing list management

- Reservations and attendance tracker

- Budget planning and reporting

- To-do lists and task management

- Word-processing capabilities, including personalized letters and envelopes, mailing labels, name tags, and biographies and personal histories

- Import/export capabilities with other spreadsheet, database, and word-processing programs

Figures 5.6 and 5.7 show pages from Minutiae Software's Reunion Planner 5.0.2, demonstrating that much of the time-consuming paperwork is automated, allowing for

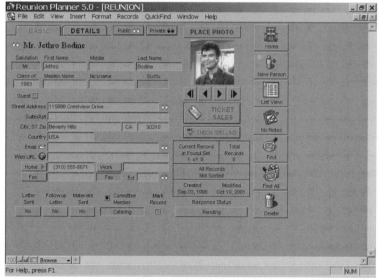

Figure 5.6 Directory screen of Reunion Planner 5.0.2

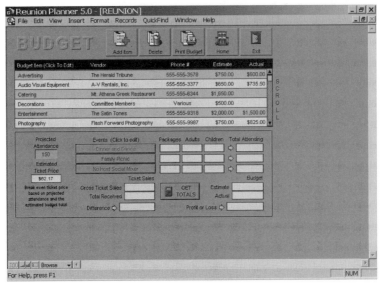

Figure 5.7 Budget screen of Reunion Planner 5.0.2

quick analysis and planning based on easy-to-retrieve summaries and reports. Many reunion software programs have Web sites where you can learn more about their features, including Reunion Planner 5.0.2 *(www.minutiaesoftware.com/reunion.htm)*, Family Reunion Organizer *(family-reunion.com/organizer)*, and Reunited! *(www.efourtech.com/reunited/reunited.htm)*.

Genealogy Software

In the 1980s, I inherited boxes of papers and file cards from my cousin Ellen, who had collected family data for decades. All of the information was either handwritten or typed. There was no central filing system, no index, no order to the records. I left those boxes untouched for several years before I dared even try to sort them out and evaluate them. Not until I bought my first personal computer in 1986 and discovered genealogy software did the task become possible. Since then, of course, I have upgraded to newer and more powerful computers and software programs, and I now have a personal family history database exceeding twenty thousand individuals in a program called The Master Genealogist. The work to date includes over eleven hundred direct ancestors dating back several hundred years and their descendants to the present day. Figure 5.8 shows you one screen of many available in The Master Genealogist.

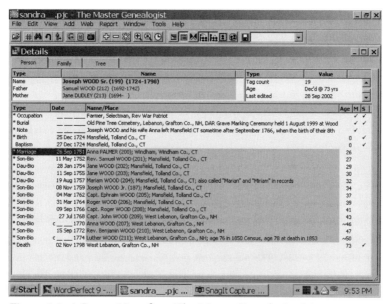

Figure 5.8 A Person View from The Master Genealogist 5.0

Many other programs are available—some free and most at modest cost. Explore the possibilities, and find the one that best meets your needs. User groups in many metropolitan areas provide instruction and support, and many software programs sponsor free e-mail lists for their users to share tips, tricks, and solutions to problems. Check the suggestions at *www.cyndislist.com/software.htm* for resources.

The information collected on family members' personal history as a result of our

When a genealogy software program is reviewed for the National Genealogical Society's *NGS NewsMagazine*, it is compared with other programs in a "Genealogical Software Report Card," which you can find online at *www.mumford.ca/reportcard/*. Different users want and need different features in a genealogy program. The "Genealogical Software Report Card" is a handy way to compare features of several genealogical software programs.

family reunions allowed me to create a variety of reports and charts. I was able to produce a personalized memory book of Wood family history back to the first immigrant ancestor in that line, born in 1598 in England. (See more details about this project in Chapter 13.)

Creating History

One reason for keeping good records is to simplify the coordination and communication for your reunion. Another is to provide future generations with a glimpse into the past. Some families have been meeting regularly for generations, and many have preserved records of those meetings, as well as programs, photographs, and other mementos. As you see in Figure 5.9, the Dreisbach family has reunion records dating back to the early twentieth century.

We create history every day of our lives. Most of it is rather routine, and we don't think that it is memorable enough to write down. Many of our ancestors did keep diaries and record books that spelled out just those everyday events. Today one of those accounts is a treasured window into the past. My maternal grandmother, Josie

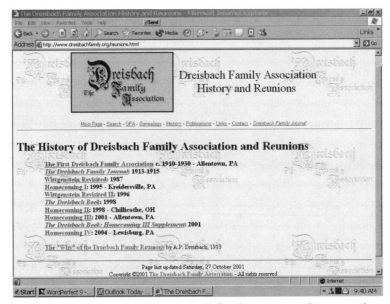

Figure 5.9 Ninety years of reunion and family association history at the Dreisbach home page

Wood Wardrobe, whom you will meet often in this book because of the words she left behind, carefully kept a record book of household expenses. While the items are indeed routine, I find it fascinating to read about the ordinary events that took place in a month such as December 1906.

On the inside covers of this record book, Grandmother wrote down the exact hour of birth—as well as the day, month, and year—for each of her four children. This information is special because no birth certificate from that time gives the hour of birth. My mother was born in November 1906, and Grandmother carefully recorded "baby weight weekly with clothes on" for the first two years of Mother's life.

Figure 5.10 shows Grandmother's household records for December 1906, a time when she had two young children. Her husband, a pharmacist who had his own drugstore, gave her thirty-one dollars each week for household expenses, including housing. She spent almost twice as much for food as for rent. She also paid almost as much for hired help as she did for rent. It's fascinating to compare these expenses with those of today. Because Grandmother was a dedicated and detailed record keeper, I have a unique glimpse into my family history.

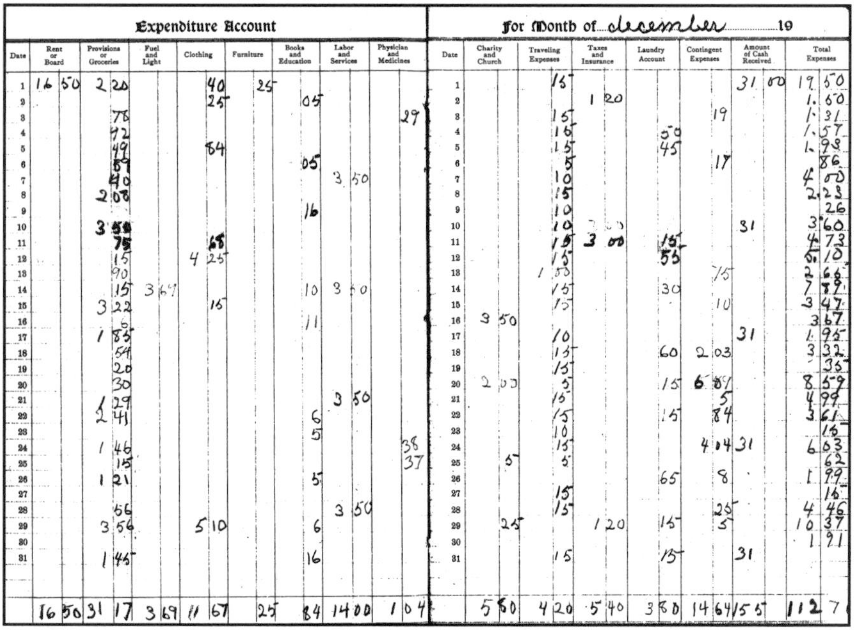

Expenditure Account

Date	Rent or Board	Provisions or Groceries	Fuel and Light	Clothing	Furniture	Books and Education	Labor and Services	Physician and Medicines
1	16 50	2 20		40	25			
2				25		05		
3		78						29
4		72						
5		49		84				
6		59				05		
7		40					3 50	
8		2 08						
9						16		
10		3 59						
11		75		68				
12		15		4 25				
13		90						
14		15	3 69			10	3 50	
15		3 22		15				
16		6				11		
17		1 85						
18		54						
19		20						
20		30						
21		1 29					3 50	
22		2 41				6		
23						5		
24		1 46						38
25		15						37
26		1 21				5		
27								
28		56					3 50	
29		3 56		5 10		6		
30								
31		1 45				16		
	16 50	31 17	3 69	11 67	25	84	14 00	1 04

For Month of december 19

Date	Charity and Church	Traveling Expenses	Taxes and Insurance	Laundry Account	Contingent Expenses	Amount of Cash Received	Total Expenses
1		15				31 00	19 50
2			1 20				1 60
3		15			19		1 31
4		15		50			1 57
5		15		45			1 98
6		5			17		86
7		10					4 00
8		15					2 23
9		10					26
10		10				31	3 60
11		15	3 00	15			4 73
12		15		55			5 10
13		1 50			15		2 66
14		15		30			7 89
15		15			10		3 47
16	3 50						3 67
17		10				31	1 95
18		15		60	2 03		3 32
19		15					35
20	2 00	5		15	6 89		8 59
21		15			5		4 99
22		15		15	84		3 61
23		10					15
24		15			4 04	31	6 03
25	5	5					62
26				65	8		1 99
27		15					15
28		15			25		4 46
29	25		1 20	15	5		10 37
30							1 91
31		15		15		31	
	5 50	4 20	5 40	3 80	14 64	155	112 7[illegible]

Figure 5.10 Josie WoodWardrobe's family expense book for December 1906

The record-keeping system that you establish for your reunion will not only facilitate your preparation and production of a memorable event, but also leave an organized collection of information to guide future reunion teams and inform future generations about your wonderful family. In the next chapter, we will explore methods of locating family members with whom you may have lost touch.

CHAPTER 6

Finding Far-flung Family

Search Methods

IT'S A CHALLENGE TO KEEP OUR HOLIDAY MAILING LISTS CURRENT THESE days. Census reports claim that up to twenty million Americans move in a given year. The young people in my family relocate so often that I used to keep their listings in pencil in my address book.

Pebble in the Pond Approach

When you toss a pebble into a pond, the ripples form circles around the point of impact. Your search for family can begin the same way. Starting with what you know, you can create ever-widening ripples. Begin with family members whose addresses or phone numbers you know. Ask them to tell you about others; soon you'll find the "information central" person, the one who keeps all the names and addresses current. In fact, each branch of the family is likely to have one of these specialists; these are the folk you want to network with in order to build the contact list. Enlisting their help involves them in the project from the start, which is a good way to develop support for the reunion. As new names accumulate, have the record keeper enter them into the database, being careful to identify family relationships. You may decide to organize reunion participants by family branches, so you should be careful to place each person in the correct branch.

Don't be discouraged with fragments of information. "I think Wally moved to

Illinois or maybe Indiana" need not be a brick wall, if you know Wally's last name or his birth date. Huge electronic databases have been established on the Internet that can assist you.

Finding Fred

Preparing for the 1994 Wood Family Reunion, I used deeds and federal census records to trace family lines down from one couple that moved to New Hampshire in 1766. One of their sons moved to northern Vermont after 1810, and little was known of his descendants. In 1994 public access was available for census films up to the 1920 census, and I found a likely family group in northern Vermont with three young sons— Robert, Donald, and Fred. I realized that in 1994, the youngest of these sons would be at least seventy-five years old. Would any still be living? In Vermont? And were they my cousins?

I wrote letters to each of them, briefly explaining that I was seeking descendants of Joseph and Anna (Palmer) Wood, and gave the line down as far as my research had taken me. I gave my address and phone number, and wrote only their names on the outside of the envelopes, which I gathered together and placed in a larger envelope addressed to the postmaster of the small town where they lived in 1920. I added a cover letter to the postmaster explaining that I was seeking to find these men for a family reunion and would appreciate the letters being forwarded to any address currently active for these families. (This would work only for a *very* small community— not somewhere like Chicago or San Francisco.)

A few weeks later, my phone rang and the caller said, "Hi, I'm your cousin Fred."

You can use the Internet to find the Post Office location nearest a given address. Go to *mapsonus.switchboard.com/db/USPS* and enter the name of the town or city and state. You will be given complete information on that post office: address, phone, hours, and even a map of the location. Interestingly, in the rural Vermont community where I located my cousins, the families' current postal addresses are in the next larger town to their village, which is itself too small to support a separate post office. And that post office address is even in a different county.

Bingo! The family group had been in that area of Vermont since 1810, the year of the deeds I had located, and the family farms were still thriving. Lucky for me, Cousin Fred, born in 1911, was the last surviving child of the 1920 family, and he provided the names and contact numbers for dozens of children, grandchildren, nieces, and nephews. Many family members from this line attended the 1994 and 1999 reunions, meeting cousins for the first time. Part of the 1999 event was an optional Sunday visit to their picturesque dairy farms, and on my departure, Cousin Fred—now nearly ninety years old—stood at the door of his farmhouse with his wife of over sixty years and cheerfully called out, "See you in 2004!"

Innovations on the Internet

People Finder Tools

In recent years, many search options have been developed in cyberspace. There are "people finder" tools and Web sites. There are databases equivalent to huge telephone books, produced by some of the nation's leading phone companies. One I use, which combines the resources of many databases, is The Ultimates *(www.theultimates.com)*, which can be searched several ways. As you see in Figure 6.1, it combines well-known database search sites, including Whitepages.com, Infospace, Yahoo PeopleFind, Switchboard, and AT&T's AnyWho. With an unusual surname, you can find every-one of that surname in the United States. For more common surnames, you can focus on a particular state. Some of the search sites provide e-mail addresses, as well. You can even get a detailed map with driving directions.

But beware: People-finder databases are often outdated. Some list my daughter with an address she held briefly eight years ago in Minnesota and a second address in Virginia that she left two years ago; both give phone numbers that have likely been assigned to other customers. Only one of these search sites provided her current phone number and the address at which she has lived for nearly two years.

Another interesting database with a reported thirty-five million names is at *www.anybirthday.com*. It is compiled from many sources, including the driver's license records of some states. If you have a name and birth date of a cousin from some family history records, plug that in and see what you can find. Chances are that few people with the same name have the same birth date.

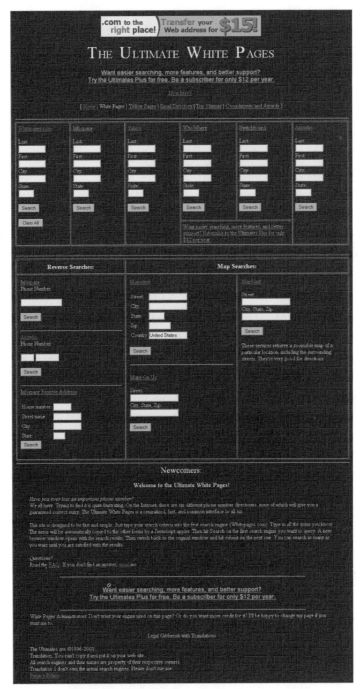

Figure 6.1 Searching many sites at once at The Ultimates

Creative Sleuthing

As a genealogist, I continue to search for ancestors and living cousins. At one Web site, I found a Web page that included some of my direct ancestors. The name of the submitter and an e-mail address was given, but my e-mails to this address were returned, indicating it was no longer an active address. Now where to look? There was no mailing address provided, the submitter had a fairly common surname, and I didn't know his birth date. Since a search at The Ultimates showed several persons of the same name in a variety of states, sending a letter to each one would not have been a wise use of time and stamps.

I went back to the genealogy Web site where I had found the information and down-loaded all the family history data, which provided the second marriage surname of the person's mother. This was a more unique name, and I searched for that name on The Ultimates site and found just one person listed. I wrote her, explaining my quest and asking that she forward my letter to her son, if indeed they fit into this family tree of mine. Within two weeks, I had an e-mail reply from him, confirming that he was a new-found cousin. He provided all his current contact numbers and offered to send me family contact information on his branch of the family for our next Wood Family Reunion.

For more information on using the Internet to find cousins, see another book in the NGS series: *Online Roots: How to Discover Your Family's History and Heritage with the Power of the Internet* by Pamela Boyer Porter, CGRS, CGL, and Amy Johnson Crow, CG.

Mail Lists

While e-mail is an important tool to use for many aspects of research, mail lists are also helpful. E-mail connects one person to another or to a group of people chosen by the person sending the message. Mail lists are more public, in that the message sender cannot control the number of recipients. And while a mail list is usually free, one must subscribe to receive the messages. In most cases, a clear mechanism is available to unsubscribe, should you decide that participation on that list is no longer helpful.

Mail lists exist for every conceivable topic of interest to human beings; the total number must be in the millions by now. All these "publications" vary in style and substance. At *www.cyndislist.com/mailing.htm,* you can find a good description and explanation of how to use mail lists. Dedicated volunteers who maintain Genealogy Resources on the Internet at *www.rootsweb.com/~jfuller/internet.html* have created and keep current a list of genealogy and history mail lists available free to the online community.

Online Forums and Message Boards

E-mail is one way of sending and receiving messages and information. It flows between two persons or among a group of selected persons chosen by the sender. To reach a larger audience, but without the same confidentiality or controls offered by e-mail, you can surf the Internet to locate online forums and message boards that may help you.

Online forums and message boards allow two-way communication. Like mail lists, these are usually free sites that have been created to facilitate the exchange of information. You can leave messages and receive messages that will be read by all users of that message board. Placing a message on a message board or forum in the form of a question is called a "query." Sometimes the messages directed to you in reply to a query may appear only at that Web site—or they may be sent to your own e-mail mailbox. The guidelines for individual forums or boards are usually posted on their first or "home" page.

> When you post a query on an online forum or message board, list only one surname in the message header, and CAPITALIZE just the surname for emphasis. Be specific and brief. Provide your e-mail address inside the message.

While planning for a reunion, you will have lots of interests to explore. For instance, to search for other relatives, you may want to find forums for the surname(s) in your family groups. Two good places to start are *www.ancestry.com* and *genforum.genealogy.com,* where you enter the surname of interest and see where that takes you.

You might head a message "John & Mary (Smith) Jones, Carter Co., TN 1880" if the contents state the family names, locations, and dates. When you place relevant information briefly in the header or subject line of the message, those who scan for headers only will know whether this message relates to their interests. Inside the message, you can expand a bit: "Seeking all descendants of John & Mary (Smith) Jones who lived with 7 children in Roseville, Carter Co., TN, in 1880 census. Family reunion planned for 2004." You might enter this message in at least three different topic forums or message boards to search by (1) the Smith surname, (2) the Jones surname, and (3) Carter County, Tennessee. That way you catch all those readers for any of the surname or location interests.

Another popular site with forums and message boards is RootsWeb, a free site supported by Ancestry.com. Go to the home page at *www.rootsweb.com* and click on Message Boards, where you can enter a query. You will likely also find that many areas of the RootsWeb site contain information about your family's ancestral home locations.

A rich and growing Web site is USGenWeb *(www.usgenweb.org),* started in 1996 and now staffed by volunteers in over three thousand counties around the nation who provide information about records, families, and history—one county at a time. The sites are arranged by state and then by county. Once you have selected a state and then a county, you can find information, ask questions, reply to messages, and publicize your reunion while you search for more cousins. If you think you have relatives in several counties and several states, you can place messages in all of the relevant Web sites.

Do Message Boards Really Work?

It was through a message board that I made a wonderful discovery during my search for lighthouse keepers' descendants for the huge Hatteras Keepers Descendants Homecoming in 2001. I went online to a surname message board with a new name I had just learned and was surprised to find another message there concerning the very same individual. I then exchanged private e-mails with the submitter, Linda, to learn that while both of us were personally unrelated to the family, we provided a unique and vital link.

Linda, who was from California, had purchased a small leather family-record album filled with names and dates and events at a flea market in North Carolina in the 1970s, just because she didn't want it to be discarded. She spent over twenty years trying to find the family to whom it belonged and had uploaded her own message online just a few days before I read it. Since the family's descendants were expected to attend the

Hatteras Homecoming, she graciously sent the small leather album to me to present to the family as a surprise gift. At the huge family reunion of over twelve hundred keeper kin, one small family treasure that had been lost for over thirty years found its way "home," to the delight of the family members and the cheers of the audience.

International Boards

With forums, message boards, and other Web tools, it is as easy to communicate with someone in China or Chile as it is with someone in the next town. Distant relatives living far away may not be able to attend your reunion, but they may have unique information that fills out the story of your ancestors. I communicate regularly with family history volunteers in England who have helped me enormously.

For those with interests outside of the United States, look for CanadaGenWeb *(www.rootsweb.com/~canwgw)* and WorldGenWeb *(www.worldgenweb.org),* which links to hundreds of countries around the globe. In addition to hunting for lost or new-found relatives, you can also post the first publicity about your upcoming reunion on these message boards.

Other Web Tools

There is a steady explosion of new Web sites on the Internet, with millions added each year. The best way to keep track of them is through search engines, indexes, and directories that use keywords and phrases to simplify your investigations for family information. Go to Google *(www.google.com)* and try the following:

1. Type in an ancestor's first and last names in lowercase letters within quotation marks: *"Alfred Dinmore".* This limits the search to that phrase only. If this turns up nothing of interest, try step 2.

2. Type in the surname alone, although this will probably reveal hundreds of sites that have the word in them. Unique surnames may have lots of alternative spellings as well, so you should try each of them, one at a time.

Most search engines seek out all matches for the words and then rank them so that you see the most relevant ones first. The more specific your search, the more likely you will find a manageable number of sites. For example, a search on the words *Jones family* in Google produces almost two million hits to sites where those two words can be found. If you narrow the search to *Henry Jones*, you get nearly half a million fewer hits. Placing the name in quotation marks and adding a location,—*"Henry Jones" Kentucky*—narrows the responses to eleven hundred sorted in order of relevancy. For a comparison of the current top search engines, go to the Search Engines Quick Guide at *www.infopeople.org/search/guide.html.*

Metasearch Engines

No single search engine can find everything available on a single topic, especially because it can take weeks or months for a new site to be listed at a search engine site. Metasearch engines combine several search engines at one site to increase the probability of locating a match. Dogpile *(www.dogpile.com)*, MetaCrawler *(www.metacrawler.com)*, and ProFusion *(www.profusion.com)* are some of the most popular metasearch sites.

Directories and Indexes

Another approach to finding information is to search directories and indexes. The Librarians' Index to the Internet at *lii.org/search* sets quality criteria before listing a Web site in its index. Yahoo, located at *www.yahoo.com*, and About.Com at *www.about.com* are large subject directories. For family researchers, the largest directory—mentioned often throughout this book—is Cyndi's List, found at *www.cyndislist.com*, where there are close to two hundred thousand links to Web sites providing information on topics of general and special interest.

Genealogical and Historical Societies

When trying to trace down descendants of a family who lived in a specific area in a given time, look for historical or genealogical societies in that community. They probably have records that can help you. Most societies now have a Web site and e-mail address, usually managed by loyal volunteers.

Respecting Privacy

Some people will not be a bit interested in family reunions for one reason or another. Even if you find them, they prefer not to participate. I have located several previously unknown cousins who never replied with even the slightest positive anticipation of our events. If after one mailing you receive no response, move on and save the postage.

You can continue your hunt for missing persons in your first mailings by listing the names and any other information you do know, then asking family members who receive the mailing if they know the whereabouts of the others. More detailed discussions about mailings are just ahead in Chapter 7.

CHAPTER 7

Reaching Your Audience: Communication and Promotion

EXTRA! EXTRA! READ ALL ABOUT IT! HOW WILL YOU GET THE WORD out about your family reunion? In addition to the early talks with family members, you will want to tap into many other communication channels. We'll begin with fliers or letters sent by "snail mail" and then explore e-mail and other online methods of gathering information and spreading the news of the reunion.

First Mailings

Your first mailing should include a brief cover letter describing the event, some forms to return, and a stamped self-addressed envelope to encourage a response. Figure 7.1 shows a sample cover letter. (Only on the first mailing did we pay for the return stamp—to encourage a reply. After that, recipients knew what the mailing was about and had already indicated an interest.)

Notice in Figure 7.2 that my first mailing reply form for the 1994 Wood Family Reunion offers an opportunity for the recipient to reply that no further mailings were desired. That way, I encouraged the person to send back at least one response in order to be removed from the mailing list. There's also an opportunity to reply "I don't know"; that gave people some wiggle room yet kept them on the list for future mailings.

1994 Wood Family Reunion

**Descendants of Joseph and Anna (Palmer) Wood
Original Grantees of Lebanon, NH 1766**

October 15, 1993

Dear _____

    In 1766, our mutual ancestors Joseph and Anna (Palmer) Wood moved their family by barge and oxen up the Connecticut River from their home in Mansfield, Connecticut, to become original grantees and settlers of the new town of Lebanon, New Hampshire.

    We shall gather together, 228 years later, as many of the descendants as we can find to share a memorable weekend. This will be the first Wood Family Reunion in over 50 years:

Friday, July 29, to Sunday, July 31, 1994

    We hope that you can join us and will save these dates. There will be food, fun, and fellowship for cousins of all ages—so please bring the whole family! There will be prizes and surprises and each adult attending will receive a personalized book of our Wood Family History.

    Please indicate your interest in joining us in July by returning the enclosed forms. Even if your plans cannot include attending the reunion, we would be very grateful to receive your family's information to add to our collection. There will be additional newsletters and mailings about the schedule of events for the weekend. To make it easy for you to reply, I have enclosed a stamped, self-addressed envelope.

    Our Wood family has been in New England now for over 350 years, and it's high time some of us renewed our friendships or had a chance to meet one another for the first time!

Sincerely,

My name
My address
My phone number
My e-mail address

Enclosures:
reply form, family data sheet, stamped reply envelope

Figure 7.1 First letter announcing the reunion

Wood Family Reunion

29-31 July 1994   Lebanon, NH

Preliminary Planning

☐ Yes!   Please keep me on the mailing list about the Reunion
                 We might have _____adults and _____ children
                 attending.

☐ Don't Know   Please keep me on the mailing list – not sure if we can
                 come yet.

☐ Sorry!   We won't be able to attend, and please remove our name
                 from the mailing list.

NAME: _____

(Fill in only if there are changes or corrections)
ADDRESS:
_____

NOTES:

_____

As we already have expenses and no treasury, early deposits will be appreciated!
The amount will be deposited towards your final reservation fees. Checks Payable:
"WFR Account"

Enclosed deposit: $_____
                 (Any amount is welcome!)

Stamped reply envelope is enclosed for your convenience

Figure 7.2 First reply form

Reunion Rumors Are Rampant

Since your first meeting with family members, the word has been circulating. Even before all the details as to time and place have been finalized, there has been an informal buzz about it among family groups. And buzz is what you want: you just need one person to register for the reunion to get others to follow suit.

The ancestors data form in Figure 7.3 resembles the personal data form you saw in Figure 5.2; both forms were sent out together. There is some difference in the nature of the information requested. In the ancestors form, respondents can select any couple in their ancestry as the focus. Data they provide about couples at each generation from themselves back to our mutual ancestors Joseph and Anna (Palmer) Wood may add missing data to the genealogy record for the extended family.

Expect that even siblings will provide information that doesn't match. At the Hatteras Homecoming event in 2001, I had three living sisters who could not agree on the birth and death dates for their own parents. So I entered all three sets of dates, documented which sister had provided each set, and gently suggested that they confer and come up with a single set of dates based on their records and recollections. Had I been doing more extensive research, I might have ordered birth and death certificates as other documentation, although it is likely that one of the sisters provided data for the death certificates on the parents. Since the only requirement for an invitation to that event was proof of a descent from a Cape Hatteras lighthouse keeper and we received data from over fifteen hundred people, I did not have the time or need to verify each and every date with other sources; I simply cited the source of each event with the name of the person providing the information.

For the Wood Work project, I want to have the best documentation I can find. Since several cousins or siblings may send in a form on the same couple and the specific data may well vary, it is important to have the name of the person submitting that form. That way, as I work to confirm or correct information in my genealogy database, I have the source to consult again.

You can find free downloadable family record forms at *genealogysearch.org/free/forms.html* and *www.pbs.org/kbyu/ancestors/firstseries/teachersguide/charts-records.html.* I designed

Data Sheet for Wood Family History (The Past Generations)

Describe your own family group. If you are not sure, enter data with a "?" to provide clues for further research.

A. HUSBAND:	
His birth date/place	
His death date/place, burial place	
His Father's full name	
His Mother's maiden name	
A & B's marriage date/place	
B. WIFE:	
Her birth date/place	
Her death date/place, burial place	
Her Father's full name	
Her Mother's maiden name	
Children of Husband A and Wife B: names, birth dates/places, death dates/places, marriages (Continue on back of sheet if needed)	
Other marriages of Husband A or Wife B	
Other info: military, occupation, etc.	
Source of information:	
Person providing data:	

Write any other information you choose on the back of this page.

Please return to: *[my name, address, phone, fax, and e-mail address]*

Date received:	Entered in database:	Other:

Figure 7.3 Data form for ancestors

my own record forms to fit on only one sheet of paper, as an incentive for folks to reply. When I see a multipage questionnaire in my mailbox or a form I don't understand, I often set it aside as too complicated to handle at the moment (and often never return to it). Many of the forms you find online are used by genealogists, who share a common language that is not always clear to a novice. I use them for my own genealogical work, but I wanted the forms I sent to non-genealogists to be "user friendly," which is why I designed my own for the reunion.

Snail Mail

To be sure that everyone has the same information, the publicity team should mail out all fliers, letters, and newsletters the old-fashioned way (known as "snail mail" in our age of instant communication)—and augment it by e-mail. As the database of names and addresses grows, each successive mailing list will be much larger; the way the price of stamps keeps rising, it's wise to be brief and use both sides of the paper. Figure 7.4 shows a sample schedule for mailings, which you can adapt to fit your reunion's timetable. The important thing to remember is to stay in regular touch and give people more than one opportunity to decide to attend your fabulous family reunion.

Months Ahead	Purpose of mailing	Send To
12–24	To gather ideas, helpers, contacts	List of known addresses
12–18	To announce, save date	Expanding list of addresses
6–12	Program details, early reservations	Expanding list of addresses
5	More details, another reservation form	All who did not reserve yet
3	Reminders Reservation Form	All on active list All not yet confirmed
1	Last-minute tips, reminders	All registered

Figure 7.4 Sample schedule for mailings

Return to Sender

Whoever takes on the task of gathering and disseminating information will probably use a personal address on the return address of mailings. But if the reunion is a large event, you may want to set up a post office box so that no one's home mailbox becomes overwhelmed. Since you are likely going to attempt to contact "long-lost"

2004 Wood Family Reunion
6 Main St., Ourtown, NH
12345-6789

Figure 7.5 Sample return-address label

family, use first-class postage whether you send postcards or mailings in envelopes. This way, if an address you've used is wrong, outdated, or past its forwarding-order time limit, it will come back to you for correction.

For the Wood family reunions, I have created return address labels on my computer and always include mention of the reunion on them. It's a great way to immediately distinguish your mail from all the rest of the mailbox's holdings. Figure 7.5 shows an adaptation of the return label we're using for the 2004 Wood Family Reunion.

As the mutual ancestors in the Wood family reunions were a colonial couple, living at the time of the American Revolution, I selected a public domain clip art symbol of a colonial town crier for my logo. Now that family members have come to recognize the logo, we use it in all printed materials about reunions. You also may want to poll your family to see whether there is an artist or graphic designer who would like to create an original logo for the reunion. If you decide to use a logo, choose one that is simple and scalable to different sizes. For example, a map of the hometown might look great as part of a flier, but not be easy to read on an address label. Figure 7.6 shows a successful logo used by the Donovan family. (Sites such as *www.free-graphics.com* and *www.clip-art.com* have free, public-domain clip art online.)

You may see an attractive image on the Internet, but don't assume it is free to use. Most Web sites clearly state their copyright notice and use policy. Some sites with graphic art state which images are copyright-free—in the "public domain"—and which are currently copyright-protected and cannot be used without express permission. Every Web screen shot printed in this book was included only after specific written permission was requested and received from the owners of that Web site.

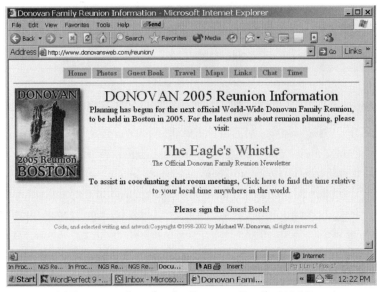

Figure 7.6 The unique logo for the Donovan Family 2005 Reunion

Tips on Addresses

Even though the United States Postal Service wants us to use the ZIP+4 codes for faster delivery, many of the addresses you collect from family members may not include the +4 codes. To update your address list, simply go online to *www.usps.com/zip4* and enter the street address, city, and state—this will display the full ZIP+4 code.

For our first mailings, I decided to address recipients by hand—just to personalize the effect. Subsequent mailings were simplified by generating labels from the computer database. Family members now recognized the return labels with the logo and knew that exciting news was inside.

E-mail

There is no quicker and more efficient way to send a message to one person or to a designated group of people than by e-mail. Most systems allow you to create special groups that can be addressed with one click. The entire reunion team can discuss details, make decisions, and confirm commitments in a moment's time. And you can send quick e-mail updates to all family members who are online. To make sure you have everyone's e-mail address, include a line asking for the e-mail address in all the forms you send to reunion participants.

Keep E-mail Healthy

We hear a lot of horror stories about computer viruses and the havoc they can wreak on the unsuspecting user. E-mail alone, the messages themselves, cannot transmit a virus. These ugly and destructive bugs and worms reside only in attachments—those extra files that someone sends *along with* a message.

A virus cannot appear on your computer all by itself. It is spread only by sharing infected files or diskettes or by downloading an infected file from the Internet. Most new computers come with some virus protection software installed. You can protect yourself and your family from contamination in many ways:

- Obtain and *use* a virus-scan program, and update it regularly.

- Make regular backups of all important information on your computer.

- Scan all files you download from the Internet and all attachments you receive in e-mail *before* you open them. This applies even to people you know. Anyone can unknowingly send an infected file.

Organize Your E-mail

Just as it's hard to extract the one piece of paper you need from a jumbled pile on your desk, it's a challenge to find a particular e-mail message you have received unless you know just where to find it—unless you've organized your online documents and filed your messages into folders or subdirectories. It will certainly be easier to find that e-mail message from Cousin Mark with the details for reserving the banquet room if you have a folder called "Banquet Room" than if it were just tossed into the general e-mail inbox that contains four hundred messages from everyone about everything. Make directories for the reunion in both your word-processor and e-mail programs.

Figure 7.7 shows how I organized my e-mail directories. (The hierarchical structure for my documents

Figure 7.7 E-mail directories

and files in the word-processor program is more extensive.) As you see, I have kept all the messages from the 1999 reunion as I work on 2004. I made categories on different aspects of the planning and even subdivided some into another layer such as the DAR marker, which involved communications with different people than did the general cemetery service. As the food items involved not only the caterer but also messages about other refreshments to be purchased and delivered to the reunion location, I separated that section. As the 2004 plans grow, I will no doubt expand the categories to include topics specific to that event.

As I continually receive messages from relatives updating family information, I have separate folders by year for those messages, under the category "New Data." These are printed out for entry into the genealogy program, but it's always good to have a backup on the computer. By backing up archived e-mails to another drive—a Zip drive or CD drive—as well as regularly backing up all important computer files to safe storage, I am protecting the information in many ways.

Your Own Web Site

If you have a high-tech relative in your planning group, perhaps you can enlist help in creating a family Web site. I went to *www.myfamily.com,* a secure site at MyFamily.com, and created the Wood family site before the 1999 reunion. Today, it is still active, with family members from all over the country participating by sharing news, photos, and other family history. MyFamily.com also provides paid subscriber services for some of its research sites and for upgraded family Web sites. But there is no charge for the basic family Web site, and it is "secure" because it is invitation-only. The whole world does not have access to your family Web site—just your own invited relatives and guests. You or one of your team members can become the "site administrator"; then you invite other family members with e-mail addresses to join.

To learn more about creating your own family history Web site, be sure to look for another book in the NGS series, *Planting Your Family Tree Online: How to Create Your Own Family History Web Site* by Cyndi Howells, creator of Cyndi's List.

You need know absolutely nothing about Web pages to create a site at MyFamily.com; all you have to do is enter information when directed, and follow simple directions to upload photographs (which are then automatically formatted for you). Figure 7.8 shows you a sample from the photo pages of my Wood family Web site.

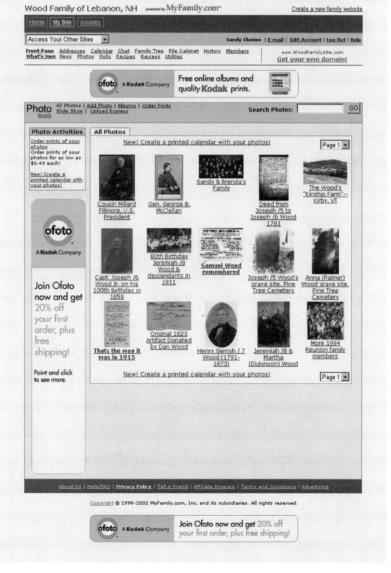

Figure 7.8 A photo page at the Wood family Web site

Two smaller sites, *www.familybuzz.com* and *www.comehome.net,* also provide family Web pages and online meeting places. Many families have created their own Web sites on the public access Web. You can find those by using a search engine with the query *"family reunion"* (use the quotation marks to limit the search to sites where the two words appear together). Family Reunion List *(www.reunionindex.com)* also offers a free Web page for posting notices of family reunions.

As you see in Figure 7.9, the Donovan family *(www.donovansweb.com/reunion)* created an online reunion registration form so that anyone with Internet access could sign up for news of the next reunion and offer their help and ideas. In Figure 7.10, the Vardiman Web site *(vardiman.treespot.net)* includes the reunion program, which shows creative ideas such as a wilderness trail walk, an archaeological project, and a 1700s dance with traditional desserts of that time.

The Armer family Web site *(www.armerfamily.com),* shown in Figure 7.11, features several innovative ideas, including a world map to indicate all the countries from which people have logged onto their site, a message board, and a reunion evaluation online form.

With all these ideas to use to tell the world about your family reunion, you can be assured that the word will get around. Maybe you'll need a larger location to hold everyone you find who wants to come! Now let's move on to two more big ingredients for a successful reunion production—choosing where everyone will sleep and what they'll eat.

| Home | Photos | Guest Book | Travel | Maps | Links | Chat | Time |

GUEST BOOK

Please let us know if you would like to come to the next reunion and/or if you would like to help with the organization or attend the planning meetings. Any help you might provide is greatly appreciated. We will send you information about the next reunion only if you so desire. We will not sell, give away, or otherwise provide your information to anyone for any purpose other than to provide you with information about Donovan Family Reunions.

Please enter as much information as possible to help us plan the next reunion.
May we send you information about the next reunion?
◉ Yes   ○ No

Name: [ ]
EMail Address: [ ]
Address Line 1: [ ]
Address Line 2: [ ]
City: [ ]
State/Province: [ ]
Country: [United States ▼]
Zip/Postal Code: [ ]

What mode(s) of travel do you plan to use?
[ ]

Have you made travel reservations?
○ Yes   ◉ No

If so, what carrier(s) are you using?
[ ]

Are you interested in sharing travel plans with other attendees (in addition to your own party)?
○ Yes   ◉ No

Have you made lodging reservations?
○ Yes   ◉ No

If so, at which place(s) of lodging?
[ ]

Do you need assistance in making travel or lodging arrangements?
○ Yes   ◉ No

Will you require special assistance or accommodations?
○ Yes   ◉ No

If so, please explain:
[ ]

What activities, events, and other items of interest would you like more information about or would like to have included in the next reunion?
[ ]

Would you like to volunteer to help organize or perform some service for the next reunion?
○ Yes   ◉ No
If so, how would you like to help?
[ ]

Comments / Questions
[ ]

[Send] [Reset]

Figure 7.9 Donovan online registration

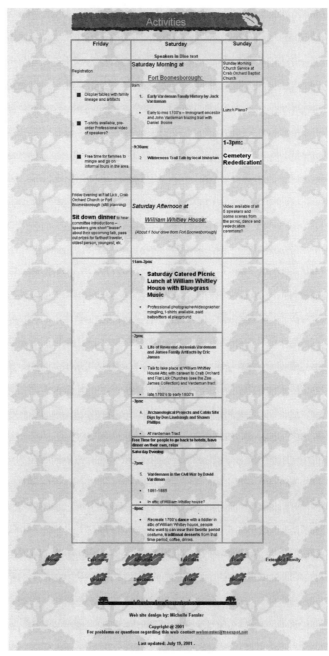

Figure 7.10 Vardiman Reunion program online

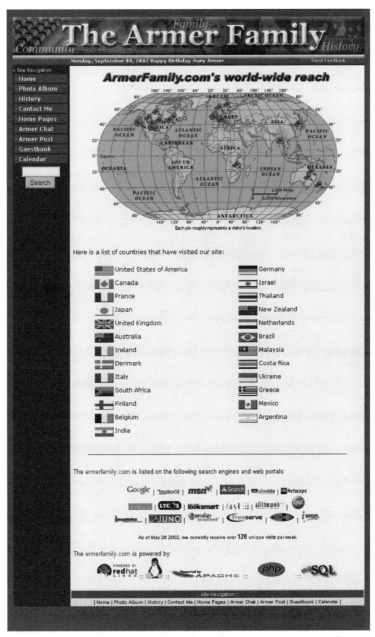

Figure 7.11 Map at the Armer family Web site, showing nationalities of visitors to the site

CHAPTER 8

Intermission and Refreshments

FOR MANY FAMILIES, THE MOST MEMORABLE REUNION EXPERIENCE IS visiting with relatives they have not seen for a while and meeting new cousins. After that, the components of an unforgettable event are great overnight accommodations and great food. Whether your reunion is just a one-day affair or a weekend event, the care and effort you make in choosing a tasty menu and offering a variety of accommodations are of utmost importance.

Sweet Dreams: Lodging

A face-to-face meeting with the manager of the accommodations you are considering reaps certain rewards:

- Learning about discounts and other amenities not usually advertised
- Touring the site and seeing sample rooms
- Connecting a face to a name, which improves communications and makes negotiating terms easier

So if at all possible, send a member of your production team to scout for information on all the hotels and motels within a reasonable distance of the actual reunion location. If there is no opportunity to make an onsite visit, gather information on accommodations from the Web by typing into a search engine the word *lodging,* along with the name of the reunion city.

Hotels and Motels

If the rates and terms are very reasonable, you may decide to select just one hotel or motel for the entire reunion. But most people like a choice, and some have special needs—mobility challenges, a cherished pet traveling companion, minimal noise, budget concerns. No single lodging option is likely to address all of them. For my Wood family reunions, I proposed a range of options (shown in Figure 8.1) with contact numbers for people to make their own reservations. I listed where I would be staying and padded that possibility by reminding folks that this particular motel was built on farmlands granted to our family in 1766 by the king of England and occupied by them for almost two hundred years. Even though this facility had no swimming pool, guess where most people stayed!

Figure 8.2 is a checklist for hotels holding a block of rooms that you have reserved. You can use this list for contract negotiations, including the all-important issue of rate. You'll also want to determine the date after which the hotel will release the unreserved rooms from your block to the general public. This "release date" is important for your timetables—family members who decide at the last minute to

Price Range	Name, Location, and Phone	Discounts and Features
From $50 +7% VT tax	Best Western at the Junction White River Junction, VT 1-800-xxx-1234	Pets welcome Fitness center Outdoor pool
From $65 +8% NH tax	Airport Economy Inn West Lebanon, NH 1-800-xxx-1234 (Sandy is staying here.)	Pets welcome Free cont. breakfast (Site is former Wood family property.)
From $85 +8% NH tax	Days Inn Lebanon, NH 1-800-xxx-1234	10% discount for AAA & AARP Free cont. breakfast
From $109 +8% NH tax	Residence Inn Lebanon, NH 1-800-xxx-1234	All suites Indoor pool Free cont. breakfast
From $26 +7% VT tax	Pine Valley RV Resort White River Junction, VT 1-800-xxx-1234	Pets welcome 90 sites, 49 with full hookups

Figure 8.1 Lodging options for the Wood Family Reunion

Checklist for Hotels

- ☐ How many rooms are reserved?
- ☐ What time period is blocked?
- ☐ Verify check-in times.
- ☐ Confirm rates.
- ☐ Are there any cancellation fees?
- ☐ Confirm that all amenities promised are available.
- ☐ Is a hotel shuttle available?
- ☐ Is there handicapped accessibility?
- ☐ Sign contract, pay deposit.

Figure 8.2 Checklist for hotels

attend the reunion may not be able to secure rooms at that hotel at the reunion rate, or even at all, if the hotel has since filled. Therefore, even if you have decided to engage only one hotel, it's wise to have a few back-up sites selected, to which you can refer late-registering family members who cannot be accommodated at the primary location.

Some hotels offer a "perk" for groups staying with them, such as a free hospitality suite. Rather than being based on the number of rooms that are used, hotels base these bonuses on "room nights," which means one room used for one night. If one room is used for two nights, that equals two room nights. When you have a group of people staying at one hotel for a weekend, the room nights add up quickly. Be aware, however, that committing to a large number of room nights brings its own risks. Say you reserve fifty rooms, and then find that you need only thirty. The hotel may charge an "attrition fee" or cancellation fee to cover its loss. This fee will appear in the contract, so keep an eye open for it and see how negotiable it is.

Whether everyone is staying at the same hotel or scattered about town, ask if you can leave small prepared "welcome packages" at the front desk to be given to each family as it checks in. This could be as simple as a large envelope, decorated with the reunion logo, that contains a welcome note, brief schedule of events, map of local attractions, and any last-minute changes.

RV Campsites

The lodging options form you saw in Figure 8.1 includes a nearby RV park. Many people today travel the country in recreational vehicles, carrying their own bed-and-breakfast with them, and others enjoy tent or cabin camping in season. If such facilities exist near your reunion site, include them in your onsite visits. A directory of campsites, together with maps and a complete list of services available at each campground, can be found at *www.reserveamerica.com*. Important items to confirm include these: Do they provide full hook-ups or partial hook-ups to electricity, water, and sewage? What is the pet policy? Are there cabin and tenting options? Supply stores? A swimming pool or playground? If several families reserve together, can they have adjoining spaces?

It's wise to make reservations for these sites well in advance in order to ensure that space is available. Each facility will have a date each year after which reservations for the next year are open.

Playing Chauffeur

If some families arrive by plane or train and do not or cannot rent cars, you'll have to arrange for pickup and for car pools to ferry them from their hotel or motel to the reunion locations. Local family groups are usually happy to volunteer for these tasks, as it gives them an extra chance to mingle with long-distance cousins.

Greet 'n' Eat: Food and Menus

My earliest memories of holiday gatherings are filled with the smells and tastes of special foods. When you think about the words "family gathering," you likely also have strong memories of wonderful aromas and images of people sharing a meal. A big part of reunion planning includes deciding how you will feed the folks. Those concerns drive many of your decisions: the timeframe of the reunion, how many meals will be shared together, and the budget. Let's look at the common ways meals and menus are developed for reunions.

Sip 'n' Snack

Besides full meals, plan to provide snacks and beverages during the entire event—usually in the hospitality suite. If you are using a hotel, check for any regulations concerning bringing in snack foods—the contract may prohibit that. But at community centers, other facilities, and park pavilions, there can be a table near the registration with the self-service snacks you select.

Don't put the snacks all out at once, lest early nibblers deplete the supplies. Instead, refresh the table as the need arises. You might want to consider individual prepackaged items like yogurt containers and granola bars, as a sanitary solution to small children with dirty hands digging into a bowl of popcorn or a plate of brownies!

Popular Snacks

- Granola bars
- Small containers of fruit yogurt (kept chilled)
- Miniature bagels (with containers of cream cheese)
- Small or large soft pretzels (with containers of mustard)
- Whole fresh fruit

A variety of beverages, hot and cold, alcoholic and nonalcoholic (more about alcohol later) should be at the ready, such as bottled water, juice, regular and diet soft drinks, regular and decaffeinated coffee and tea, and red and white wine. Soft drinks in cans need no extra supplies, except possibly a straw, and can be stored in tubs of ice. (A new trash can makes a good container.) Two-liter bottles are less costly, but you then need cups—and extra ice since larger bottles can't be returned to a tub of ice. Don't forget to respect the local recycling regulations and separate cans or plastic bottles from paper discards.

One Day or Weekend Event

Family meals can range from simple outdoor picnics and elegant evening dinners to a banquet at a hotel. They may be prepared and served by a reunion team, assembled from contributions brought by families, or catered by an outside provider. It's all up to you and your team. The Wood Family Reunion weekends have developed to include the following meals:

- Friday night: optional dutch-treat get-together at a restaurant

- Saturday: all-day snacks and a main catered meal in the early afternoon

- Sunday morning: optional dutch-treat breakfast at a hotel restaurant

Our team selects a caterer for Saturday and restaurants for the Friday evening and Sunday morning meals. Registration forms include check-off boxes for those planning to attend the Friday or Sunday meals, so that approximate numbers can be relayed for a reservation. We had so many family members register for the Sunday breakfast at the last reunion that the hotel offered us a private dining room. We got to fill our plates from a sumptuous buffet in the main restaurant, then bring our meals back to the private room, where a juice and coffee bar had been set up. I expected only out-of-towners to gather for these optional meals, so I was surprised when many of the local families also enjoyed the extra events, which happily provided them with more time to visit their long-time and new-found cousins.

Be sure the menus are varied enough to accommodate those with special dietary needs or preferences. You can inquire about special needs on registration forms, but plan anyhow to include a variety of meat-free protein items and sugar-free desserts.

Let Others Do It All

If you have selected a facility other than a hotel, such as a community center, church hall, or—as we did for one Wood reunion—a ski lodge, you should probably locate an outside provider for your meals. The checklist in Figure 8.3 covers the basics that can guide you in your deliberations and negotiations. Serving meals this way isn't simple. In addition to a set rental fee by the hour or day, there may be fees for a variety of other items, such as tables and chairs, use of a facility's kitchen for food preparation, and extra time to set up and clean up. Make sure you determine these additional costs. Does the facility have a list of approved caterers, or may you hire your own? In the case of a church or fellowship hall, an auxiliary group associated with it may prepare and serve meals for separate fees.

Your reunion may be scheduled from 10 A.M. to 5 P.M., but you need time before and after for setup and cleanup, as mentioned above. Consult with the facility, and check the agreement you sign and all its terms and conditions very carefully. Is extra time allotted for setup and cleanup? You don't want to have another group lined up at the door at 5 P.M., anxious to get ready for the square dance being held there that evening.

Checklist for Community Facilities Other Than Hotels

☐ What is the site rental fee?
☐ Are there any additional fees?
☐ How many hours are included in the rental, including setup and cleanup? Are additional hours possible?
☐ Does the facility have a list of approved caterers, or may you hire your own?
☐ Is there an onsite kitchen that can be used?
☐ Is there handicapped accessibility?
☐ Sign contract, pay deposit.

Figure 8.3 Checklist for community facilities

Figure 8.4 provides a checklist to use when hiring a caterer. In addition to getting estimates and proposals from more than one, do check the references they provide from customers who have used their services. Obviously, caterers will not refer you to former customers who were unhappy with their work, but you can ask former clients your own questions: "What was the most positive aspect of using this caterer?" "What was the biggest challenge in working with them?"

Checklist for Caterers

☐ Get "per person" estimates.
☐ Read the policy on deposits and cancellations.
☐ Check recent references.
☐ Set up sample tastings.
☐ Is the caterer familiar with the reunion site? If not, have the caterer visit to assess needs.
☐ Choose menus and format (sit-down, buffet).
☐ Sign contract, pay deposit.
☐ Finalize menus.
☐ Include any special dietary needs.
☐ Provide a final head count.
☐ Make a final check on menus, seating, table arrangements.
☐ Settle final payment method.

Figure 8.4 Checklist for caterers

If possible, hire a catering firm that is familiar with the facility you have selected. If they have not worked at that site before, make sure they visit it before you sign a final contract, so they can determine whether the facility kitchen has all the equipment they need or whether they will have to charge extra to bring their own.

Buffet service can be an inexpensive way to cater a lovely meal. With staff behind the buffet table, serving as guests pass by, you'll be assured there is ample food for everyone.

Will Alcohol Be Served?

Local laws and regulations may govern this decision as much as family personal choices. Many public park sites prohibit patrons from bringing alcoholic beverages into the property. Most hotels require that bartenders be hired to serve even beer and wine, which will add an expense to your budget. During the survey and planning process, ask family members about their preferences. It's important to be considerate of the views of the attendees, and some may prefer a nonalcoholic beverage menu when there are many children present.

At our reunion held at the ski lodge off-season, the contract permitted us to bring in soft drinks, tubs, and ice but required a facility-provided bartender be hired to sell beer and wine. We contracted for four hours of services from noon to 4 P.M. at ten dollars an hour. All sales receipts went to the facility. As I recall, there was little interest in the wine, but the unexpected ninety-degree day in a building without air-conditioning did attract some adults to the cold beer option.

Do It Yourself—Potluck

The term "potluck" once applied to providing whatever food happened to be available for a meal. Today, a "potluck supper" has come to mean a meal at which each guest brings food that is shared by all. The menu is planned in advance, and people either volunteer for or are assigned to bring a certain item. If you decide to go potluck offsite, find out who the renowned cooks are in your family, and who has special dish memories—via the reunion registration form. I can still vividly recall the smell and taste of my grandmother's freshly baked breads and rolls. Each Thanksgiving, my sister and I—now grandmothers ourselves—enjoy our servings of butternut squash and creamed onions. These are dishes that no one else in the family cares to taste, but ones that remind us of our New England childhood holiday dinners when these two vegetables were always on the table.

There may be longtime favorite family foods that you want to include, but cooking

PUMPKIN CAKE

DESSERTS

INGREDIENTS	50 SERVINGS		100 SERVINGS		SERVINGS		DIRECTIONS
	WEIGHT	MEASURE	WEIGHT	MEASURE	WEIGHT	MEASURE	
Sugar	1 lb 13 oz	1 qt	3 lb 10 oz	2 qts			1. In a mixing bowl using a paddle attachment,
Margarine or butter	8 oz	1 cup	1 lb	2 cups			cream the sugar, margarine, and salt for
Salt		1½ tsp		1 Tbsp			10 minutes at medium speed.
Canned solid pack pumpkin	2 lb	1 qt	4 lb	2 qts			2. Add pumpkin and mix for 2 minutes. Scrape
Frozen whole eggs *or*	12 oz		1 lb 8 oz				down sides of bowl.
Whole large eggs		6 ea		12 ea			
Lowfat milk	1 lb 4 oz	2½ cups	2 lb 8 oz	1 qt 1 cup			3. Slowly add eggs. Scrape down sides of bowl.
All-purpose flour	1 lb 9 oz	1 qt 1 cup	3 lb 2 oz	2 qt 2 cups			4. Slowly add milk. Scrape down sides of bowl.
Baking powder		2½ tsp		1 Tbsp 2 tsp			
Baking soda		1½ tsp		1 Tbsp			5. In a separate bowl mix flour, baking powder,
Ground cinnamon		2 tsp		1 Tbsp 1 tsp			baking soda, cinnamon, and nutmeg. Add to
Ground nutmeg		2 tsp		1 Tbsp 1 tsp			above mixture. Mix at low speed for 1 minute.

Serving: 1 piece (70 grams)

Yield: 50 servings: 7 lb 13 oz (3500 grams)
100 servings: 15 lb 12 oz (7000 grams)

Dip 3 qts 3¼ cups into each greased and floured 18"x 26"x 1" sheet pan. Bake in a conventional oven at 350°F for 35 to 40 minutes or a convection oven at 325°F for 30 to 35 minutes. Cut each cake 5 x 10 to make 50 servings.

Figure 8.5 A make-ahead dessert for fifty or one hundred servings from the U.S. Department of Agriculture

for fifty or one hundred people is quite from different cooking for a few. Just take a look at the high-yield recipe for pumpkin cake in Figure 8.5 to get an idea of the ingredient quantities involved. Quantity cooking ideas and recipes can be found on the Web at such sites as *members.tripod.com/~lotsofinfo/index.html, www.angelfire.com/bc/incredible,* and *www.hillbillyhousewife.com/quantityrecipes.htm* You'll also find guidelines to guarantee a memorable meal.

Divide up the menu among the families by courses: vegetables, salads, breads, desserts. Ask those traveling in from a distance to simply make a cash contribution for beverages or paper supplies. Your planning team should discuss all these ideas and come up with the plan that works best for your event—but don't forget to assign setup, preparation, serving, and cleanup tasks.

You can find helpful food safety tips at the National Food Processors Association Web site *(www.safefood.org/picnicfact.html).*

Better Safe Than Sorry

A few important logistical and food safety items must be considered when you prepare your own food. Food safety requires that hot foods be kept at 140 degrees Fahrenheit or above and that perishable cold foods be kept at 40 degrees or below. Meat dishes such as fried chicken, barbequed beef, or chili, and perishable salads such as potato salad should be prepared where the meal will be served, then supplemented with foods that are less likely to spoil in transit, such as vegetables, fresh fruits, breads, and desserts. Be sure you have safe food storage at the reunion site; if you're having a picnic, definitely determine the number of coolers needed and add them to the list of supplies.

Potluck also means needing big chafing dishes, large bowls, and other serving pieces. Party retail stores in urban areas often carry disposable serving pieces; that way, you don't have to remember which bowls were rented and which belong to Aunt Susan.

Hotel or Restaurant Banquet

If the reunion meals take place in a hotel or restaurant, you have additional questions to ask. (See the checklist in Figure 8.6.) Perhaps most important, in terms of ambiance: Will there be a private dining space or will you have to share the space with other patrons? As reunion dinners usually have a program with talks and awards, a shared space may not be suitable. Contract with a hotel whose ballrooms can be subdivided into two or three smaller spaces to hold concurrent group functions.

Acoustics are another issue: You don't want to meet in a ballroom section with a noisy wedding party and full orchestra on the other side of the room divider.

Checklist for Hotel or Restaurant Dinner

☐ Will there be private dining space, or will you have to share space with other patrons?

☐ Is there ample parking available?

☐ Is there handicapped accessibility?

☐ How are the acoustics?

Figure 8.6 Checklist for hotel or restaurant dinner

Remember, though, until you can confirm your final numbers for the dinner or banquet, you may not be assigned a specific room. In fact, the hotel may not assign a specific room until the day of the dinner, depending on what other groups have reserved similar spaces in that location. Therefore, your pre-event publicity should include only the name of the hotel, not the function room.

Do not assume that extra items are included in a hotel banquet contract unless they are specifically listed in your contract—including props, candles, centerpieces, upgraded china, and table linens for a formal affair. Many hotels have handsome brochures that present glamorous views of elegant functions, but these often showcase the highest-priced options. So that you aren't disappointed that the final decorations for your banquet are less than you expected, be sure to determine what's included in your specific price range. Remember, if it's not in print, it won't happen. If you establish a cooperative working agreement with the sales or banquet manager and stay in touch throughout the pre-reunion period, things should go smoothly. When personnel change, as they often do in the hotel business, meet the replacement person as soon as possible to maintain continuity.

Celebrate the Ancestors

Food is a wonderful way to celebrate your ancestors. A good way to gather together old family dishes is to make a list of all the countries from which your ancestors emigrated, and ask family members for recipes that represent those cultures. An informal reunion planning committee meeting might include taste-testing samples of these to determine which ones will appeal the most, and work well for the reunion. The results could lead to a family cookbook; read more about that idea in Chapter 15.

Tasty Timelines

You'll find interesting histories of food items, social history, manners, and menus at the Food Timeline and Culinary History Timeline *(www.gti.net/mocolib1/kid/food1.html)*, the Web site of the Morris County Library of Whippany, New Jersey.

Audience Participation

At a do-it-yourself event, a great way to engage the group is to involve them all in food preparation. How? Well, they can build a six-foot sandwich as a group. Or you can create a buffet taco bar with all the fixings in separate bowls so people can choose just what items to include in their personal taco. Another fun treat is creating an ice cream bar where people make their own sundae, with a variety of toppings. Don't forget some low-fat or non-fat frozen yogurt for those who prefer a healthier alternative.

Ice Cream Surprise

At a number of reunions, I have reserved an ice cream truck in advance, ordered the number and selection of products, and prepaid for the whole order as part of the event. The ringing bell of the ice cream truck never fails to cause an instant scramble to line up for treats—with adults as often as not at the head of the line.

Carefree Cookouts

Picnics and cookouts can feature a simple menu—hot dogs, hamburgers, corn on the cob, watermelon—or more sophisticated fare, like grilled salmon and steaks, special salads, fresh breads, and elegant desserts. Grill chefs who can cook to order are key to making this outdoor event work—so survey family members on the registration form or by e-mail. In hot weather, it's wise to schedule chefs at the grill for no more than twenty minutes per shift, as it can get mighty uncomfortable standing over the hot coals. The food team can plan, order, and bring all the food and supplies for grilling and serving.

Prepare for unwanted insect guests with supplies of citronella candles; net "umbrellas" to cover serving bowls of food; a small first-aid kit with bandages, sanitizing wipes, sunblock, and soothing treatments for bug bites; and lots of disposable towelettes and a liquid sanitizer. Always expect the unexpected: The success of any outdoor event depends on the weather. An unseasonably hot weekend means thirstier guests. A sudden shower may not dampen spirits, but may dampen the pastries if shelter is not available quickly.

In this chapter, you have learned how to make arrangements to lodge and feed the reunion crowd. Next we'll explore the wide range of activities that you can plan to keep everyone engaged. Attending to these details ensures that there will be plenty of food, fun, and fellowship on your big day.

CHAPTER 9

Audience Participation

ALTHOUGH A BIG PART OF A FAMILY REUNION IS PEOPLE TALKING together—catching up, reminiscing, and getting to know each other—you and your team should organize a variety of activities to occur throughout the reunion. You need *not* run a three-ring circus, but planned activities provide an easy way for people who do not know each other well to quickly find a comfort level. A reunion program that specifies how the reunion events will unfold is a good thing to include as a handout on arrival, for it gives the relatives a current picture of the day's or weekend's events. (See Figure 9.1 for the program from the last Wood Reunion.)

The Sound of Music

Whether it's a CD boom box hooked up to speakers, a full-fledged family orchestra, or nostalgic sing-alongs, music is always welcome at group gatherings. At a large, multi-generational event, you're likely to have people who remember "their songs" from all the decades of the latter twentieth century, so gather up some tapes or CDs that provide Best Hits of the 1940s, '50s, '60s, and so on—and ask reunion participants to bring some of their own favorites. (Just make sure each disk is labeled with the owner's name so it gets back to the right person.) At *www.1960sflashback.com/1960/Music.asp*, you can find collections from the 1960s through the 1990s, and this Web site links to the huge *www.Amazon.com* site, where you can search for additional music.

117

1999 Wood Family Reunion
July 30-31, August 1, 1999

Program of Events
(maps on reverse side)

Friday evening, July 30

5:00-7:00 P.M.	Informal Gathering lobby of Airport Inn
7:00 P.M.	Dutch-Treat Dinner option Alberti Restaurant (walking distance)

Saturday, July 31   Lebanon Ski Lodge

10:00 A.M.	Registration
10:30-12:30	Games, Contests, Exhibits
12:30-1:30 P.M.	Catered Luncheon
2:00 P.M.	Group Photo
3:00 P.M.	Prizes and Surprises

Sunday morning, August 1

8:30 A.M.	Breakfast Buffet option Sheraton Hotel
10:30 A.M.	DAR Grave-Marking Ceremony for Joseph Wood Pine Tree Cemetery
11:30 A.M.	Optional tours

Figure 9.1 Wood Reunion program

Sing-alongs

Sing-alongs may be silly—but they're also fun. If a piano is available and someone who can play it is in your audience, so much the better. Otherwise, there are CDs and tapes with background music for sing-alongs. Let the MTV generation participate in old-fashioned rounds like "Row, Row, Row Your Boat," "Frère Jacques," and "Three Blind Mice," where the whole group is divided into sections. You can find more song ideas on the Web. Go to *www.geocities.com/EnchantedForest/Glade/8851/songs3.htm* and *www.niehs.nih.gov/kids/home.htm,* a federal government collection of children's songs and games from the National Institute of Environmental Health Sciences.

Song and Dance

The polka, square dance, hora, contradance, and line dance are traditional dances that everyone can enjoy. Try to plan in advance to ensure that the appropriate music to accompany these dances is available on tape or CD—ready for when the dancing spirit moves through the reunion.

Family Talent Show

For a show within a show, think about a family talent show. Here's how Bobbi King described her Hytrek Family Reunion:

> Talent may be an expansive use of the word, but the family talent show gathers us together. Our kids can show off their talents, we hear families sing in harmony or in solo voice, and we have some remarkable musical surprises. One set of cousins put together a country western salute in song and dance for us. We have discovered fiddle players and guitar pickers. Most of the kids love getting up in front of the crowd, and you can count on appreciative applause. We have heard terrible jokes, watched lame skits, and groaned at off-key singing, but the talent show remains an important focal point of our reunions.

Have your stage manager, the creative person responsible for organizing many of the reunion's events, contact families ahead of time to line people up. That way, family groups or individuals have a chance to plan, rehearse, and bring whatever props or costumes they need. Or schedule an "open mic" time and invite people to perform (you might want to have a couple of prearranged performances to warm up the crowd so that others will want to jump up and join the fun).

Keeping Kids Involved

Children love to compete for prizes, so make sure to include lots of them. But there should be no losers at a reunion contest—every child should receive some kind of recognition, no matter his actual ranking. I purchased dozens of ribbons at a sports store, and in addition to the typical first, second, and third prize ribbons, I was delighted to find a ribbon titled "Participant." You can also purchase ribbons for under fifty cents each online at *www.regal-ribbons.com/awribwcarbac.html* and *www.trophynthings.com/ribbons.htm*. Look for the type that has a card on the back, so it can be inscribed with the reunion name and date in advance. Then all you need to add is the winner's name, and the child has a wonderful souvenir to take home.

Make Your Own Puzzles

Figures 9.2 and 9.3 show two puzzles I created for the Wood reunion—a fun facts contest and word scramble. Using information unique to your own family, make these fun activities a learning experience as well. Kids can complete them whenever they want, and the winners are announced at the end of the day. The first prize could go to the first person to submit the most correct answers. The Fun Facts puzzle was created after registrations started coming in and we had the information on different families. The Word Scramble puzzle was designed to inform children about everyone's mutual ancestors, whom they could find by studying the charts on the wall or the memory books given to each adult.

Icebreakers and Introductions

An intergenerational audience-participation game called "Meet Our Family" is a great way to pull the group together. With a bowl of wrapped candies at the ready, ask each family member to take up to five pieces of candy—but at least two pieces. Then announce that for each piece of candy held, each person must first identify himself, and then say something about himself ("My name is Tom, and I love to play tennis"). You may want to use a microphone or horn to make sure all present can hear about their family. The contest ends when you ask for volunteers to share how many first names they can remember—the person with the most correct names wins a prize. And every participant gets a ribbon of some kind.

The Wood Family Reunion
Fun Facts Contest

Meet family members today and find out the answers to fill in the blanks. Prize for most correct answers!

1. Get names of people who live full time in the following states: (hint: check name badges)

Find **one person each** who lives full time in: (Write their name down)

California_____

Illinois_____

Indiana_____

Iowa_____

Kentucky_____

Pennsylvania_____

Virginia_____

2. Find **three people** with **different last names** who live full time in Florida:

_____

_____

_____

3. Two couples here today have been married for more than 60 years. Who are they?

_____

_____

MY NAME:_____

Figure 9.2 Family fun facts contest

The Wood Family Reunion Word Scramble

N	I	M	A	J	N	E	B
E	E	N	I	P	T	F	D
J	B	S	A	M	U	E	L
G	A	B	K	A	C	P	E
R	J	N	A	R	I	H	I
M	O	Q	E	I	T	R	F
L	S	G	R	A	C	A	S
U	E	W	E	M	E	I	N
T	P	A	M	R	N	M	A
H	H	N	L	X	N	Z	M
E	L	N	A	J	O	H	N
R	B	A	P	Y	C	R	S

Find the following words (any direction), and circle them:

Names of ten surviving children of Joseph and Anna Wood.

_____   _____   _____   _____

_____   _____   _____   _____

_____   _____

The state in which Joseph Wood was born :_____

The town in which Joseph Wood was born: _____

Anna Wood's maiden name:_____

Anna Wood's mother's maiden name: _____

Joseph and Anna are buried at _____ Tree Cemetery.

MY NAME:_____

Figure 9.3 Family word scramble

Contests for Helpers

To let children compete while contributing to the reunion, the Wood family schedules several "trash" contests. The announcer calls out the contest and hands out large trash bags to each child who wants to participate. Then a whistle is blasted to mark the start and finish of a five-minute contest to gather up as much trash as possible and take it to a central collection spot. Lest they swoop down and remove cups or plates still in use, some rules were devised, including "Ask if the person is finished with it." By the end of the day, we had very little trash left to be collected.

Story-Telling Contests

Children love to hear and tell stories: They want to hear Grandma or Grandpa tell about their parents as children; children also have good stories to tell about their own parents. Most of these are funny—some may be slightly embarrassing—and they all serve to get everyone laughing and involved.

To get the story telling started, hand out index cards with topics on them to a few adults who are willing to start off the fun. The cards could say: "When I was child, we celebrated Thanksgiving by . . ." or "When I went to visit my grandparents, I remember . . ." or "The funniest memory I have of Bob as a child is the time when . . ." or "You'd never believe it, but one time when she was about six, Veronica . . ."

Arts and Crafts Table

Unroll some butcher paper on a long table, add markers and crayons, and announce that everyone is invited to come up and add something to the "Reunion Mural"— a drawing of a family group or favorite reunion activity, for instance—and have each person sign his or her contribution. At the end of the day, display the one-of-a-kind family mural; then roll it up for the next reunion, when everyone will enjoy remembering its creation.

Another crafts table activity has participants create a family quilt. You'll need a bunch of twelve-inch squares of cloth and some permanent fabric-marking pens. The cloth pieces can be of a variety of patterns and light colors, gathered from scraps or purchased new at the bargain tables—light colors allow the individual artists' hand-drawn designs to show well. When the reunion is over, gather the squares so they can be assembled into a quilt to be raffled off—or at least proudly exhibited—at the next reunion.

Quiet and Noisy Games and Races

The young and young-at-heart will enjoy a lot of physical activity, so be sure to offer a lot of races, tournaments, and games for children of all ages to enjoy. While it's best to have as many multigenerational activities as possible so that everyone can participate, some sports, such as horseshoes, volleyball, and softball, work best for the twelve-years-and-over crowd. When you want the atmosphere to quiet down a little or should Mother Nature shower the festivities with unexpected thunderstorms, board games will fill the time until the sun shines again.

Board Games

Checkers and chess matches are always popular among all age groups, and they will also attract a small audience of lookers-on and kibitzers who will add to the fun. There are a few commercial board games designed just for family gatherings; an example is shown in Figure 9.4. If your budget allows, you might look at *shop.store.yahoo.com/tngenterprises/usaop_156.html*, *www.FunStuffForGenealogists.com*, and *www.boardgames.com/lifestories.html* for ideas and inspiration. A reminiscing game just for family members over age thirty can be found at *www.tdcgames.com/rem.htm*. If you choose to invest in some reunion board games, the cost will amortize over time, as they can be used for many reunions to come. All you need is someone to volunteer a safe and dry basement, attic, or garage for safekeeping.

Mummy Wrap

The mummy wrap contest is a hilarious crowd-pleaser. Pair off participants into two-person teams, giving each team one roll of toilet tissue. One member of the team is the "wrapper," and the other is the "mummy." At the sound of a whistle, the wrapper begins to cover the mummy—from the top down or from the bottom up, covering everything except the eyes. The first team with a full-length mummy wins the prize. Be sure to have the cameras clicking for this one.

Tug-of-War

The age-old game of tug-of-war triggers the competitive juices of many a family member. It's certainly simple enough: get some ten- to twenty-foot lengths of thick, soft rope from the hardware store, tie a colored ribbon or piece of yarn tightly in the middle of the lengths of rope, and tie a few knots in the rope to give a good grip. (Caution players that

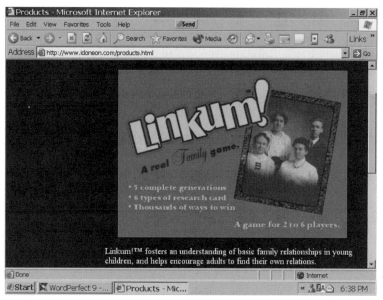

Figure 9.4 A board game for family reunions

only hands can be used and that it is dangerous to wrap the rope around a wrist or a waist.) Mark a line on the ground with tape, and match up the center of the ribbon to the marked line. Create teams, distributing sizes and weights of players evenly on both teams. Ask teams to stand about six feet back from the line. At the sound of the whistle, the fun begins as, of course, each team tries to pull the other team across the line.

You can turn this into a tournament by family group and create a bit of suspense for everyone: Draw two family names out of a hat to start, and then a new name to challenge each winner until all groups have participated. Cousins will enjoy friendly interfamily competition.

Parent-Calling Contest

The only supplies needed for the parent-calling contest are blindfolds. Moms and dads are lined up blindfolded (bandanas make good blindfolds), while their children scatter at a distance. When a whistle blows, the kids start calling out "Mom!" or "Dad!" and the parents move toward where they think their child is. (The parents keep moving, but the children stand still.) The first parent to touch his or her own child wins. If a set of parents has several children present, play several rounds of this game to include every-one. And you can reverse it—blindfold the kids and have them try to find their parents.

Three-legged Races

For rhree legged races, let family members pair up as they would like: two kids the same general size, a parent and a child, or two adults. With a short piece of soft rope, tie the right leg of one to the left leg of the other. At the sound of the whistle, they're off, running for the finish line and hoping to stay synchronized and avoid tumbles. You could vary this by tying three or four people together and seeing how that changes things.

Appropriateness and safety are two key concepts in planning activities. Make sure game surfaces have no hidden hazards. Allow no swimming without the presence of a trained lifeguard.

Sack Races

Are there any old-fashioned burlap sacks around these days? If not, try trash bags for sack races—although they may prove slippery. The standard rules are that each person gets into a bag, lines up at a starting line, and at the signal, hops to the finish line. Since safety is a prime consideration, be sure all these physical games have a safe surface on which players can run or hop. As an early task on reunion day, have a team walk the grounds with a sharp eye, scanning for any potential hazards such as rocks or glass that could cause an injury.

Wheelbarrow Races

The teams for wheelbarrow races will likely consist of a parent and child (you can guess who takes which position!). One team member (the "wheelbarrow") gets down on all fours, and the partner stands behind. At the signal, the standing partners pick up the wheelbarrow partners' legs and the teams run to the finish line, with the wheelbarrow partners running on their arms.

Elders Have Staying Power

At our 1999 Wood Reunion, the first guest to arrive and the last to leave was also the oldest person in attendance—nearly ninety! Despite unseasonable heat, she was actively involved in all the day's activities.

Specialized Outdoor Activities

If you are extending the reunion time over a long weekend and the reunion location is accessible to a lake, pond, or golf course, you might consider planning some specialized outdoor activities. Some activities, such as a golf tournament, may be geared toward adults, while others may be appropriate for the whole family.

Family Golf Tournament

A family golf tournament can be as informal or involved as you choose, depending on your goal: A pleasant afternoon of camaraderie and conversation? A game of challenge and spirited competition? Golf does require a certain amount of planning, so select someone to lead the team that surveys available golf courses. An onsite visit allows the team to meet with the course's pro-shop staff to determine fees, tee times, and other details. Early reunion mailings should include a separate sheet for the tournament and request prompt replies so the team can determine whether there are enough people interested to make it a go. Ask about individual golf handicaps and whether some long-distance travelers will need to rent clubs or shoes.

One of the most popular formats is called "Scramble." This involves putting people of various golfing abilities together in a foursome to compete as a group against other foursomes. In this way, everyone feels included and a part of the game, regardless of expertise, and each group is balanced to have at least one experienced golfer. In play, all four players in the group hit a shot from the same spot. The spot at which the best shot lands is marked. All four then hit their next shot from the spot where the best previous shot landed. Of course, the winning team is the foursome with the best score.

You can also give out special prizes such as "Best Score without a Handicap" and "Best Score with a Handicap." And consider adding fun prizes for "Not Keeping Your

Keep an eye out for Mother Nature! Have alternate plans and supplies ready in case of sudden showers. These plans might include an indoor putting contest, crafts, board games, and sing-alongs. At our 1999 Wood Reunion, an unexpected heat wave produced ninety-degree temperatures in a Vermont ski lodge without air conditioning. We found industrial-strength floor fans, which helped keep both the air and activities moving well. The tubs of iced cold drinks were replenished often with new supplies, and we didn't forget to provide sustenance to the catering staff tending the outdoor grills in the hot sun.

Eye on the Ball," "Most Improved," or "Top Junior Player" (for golfers under age eighteen, for example).

If you want more elegant prizes than ribbons for the golfers, consider adding a few dollars to the registration for the tournament to purchase them—for instance, a unique club cover to award to all players at the end of the day. Save the awards ceremony until all the golfers return to the main reunion site so you can make it a big deal with lots of cheering from the crowd.

Family Fun Fishing Tournament

Whether it's from the end of a pier or a rowboat on a lake, fishing is family fun that can be part of your reunion if the location allows it. List it on your preliminary program mailing, asking whether recipients are interested. If circumstances permit it, even the youngest children might enjoy a fishing lesson on the banks of a pond with the family "experts." Local laws and regulations may come into play with this activity, including requirements for fishing licenses. If so, arrange for the anglers to get their licenses by mail ahead of time, or look for a place that allows one-day fishermen to try their luck, with no license required.

While specialized activities, such as golf or fishing tournaments are fun, you need to be sure to include as many family members as possible in reunion events. Plan a variety of activities for all ages and for those with diverse interests, and add some of the old-fashioned favorites. However, don't fill every single moment with things to *do*. Remember to leave plenty of time for folks simply to *be* together.

CHAPTER 10

Setting the Stage

AT A BROADWAY SHOW, THE SET DECORATOR, ART DIRECTOR, AND COSTUME designer are invisible to the audience. Their names appear on programs in small print, but their work influences the whole production in a major way. For your reunion production, these activities take on a similarly important role. You can spend weeks organizing exhibits of photos, heirlooms, and artifacts (see Chapter 11), but if the family members can't find their way around the exhibits, can't easily identify new-found cousins, or don't know when the different events are taking place, the reunion simply won't be as enjoyable as it could have been.

Set Design and Decoration

You've already chosen the "set" for your reunion: a grassy park, a hotel ballroom, a local community center. Your production must be designed based on both the opportunities and the limitations of the site you select. While a large hotel or community center hall can provide lots of wall space for decoration and guaranteed dry table space for mounting exhibits, you have to be more innovative at the park pavilion. Perhaps there you can erect a small tent for reunion exhibits, hang decorations from trees—even put reunion signs on garbage cans!

Right This Way: Signs

Even if you have included maps in your final mailing or have directed drivers to such sites as *www.mapblast.com, maps.yahoo.com,* or *www.mapquest.com,* where they can obtain both maps and driving directions from point to point, there are still helpful ways to make sure arriving guests can find you. Most hotels have sign boards in or near the lobby to direct people to the events taking place there. At a rural reunion site, you might place a bunch of colorful helium-filled balloons at the nearest entrance. With a fat marker, write one or two large words on each balloon such as "Wood Family," "Reunion,"and "Welcome!" If there is no nearby post to which you can affix the balloon bunch, add longer strings and tie them around a brick or a cinder block to stand alone at the entrance.

If you need to organize parking for a field, assign a few young volunteers to serve as guides during the arrival time, so that cars can be parked in an orderly way to allow easy access and exits. These can be the first greeters to welcome new arrivals and point them in the right direction. Make certain they wear orange safety vests or bright clothing or carry bright-colored wands so they can be easily seen and identified as traffic guides.

Programs

You and your team will develop a reunion program during the preparation period and include it in mailings as the time for the big day approaches. When guests arrive to register, hand them a fresh copy of the final program, not only as a guide, but as a souvenir as well.

Make the program as simple or as elaborate as your time and talents allow, but be certain to include *what* is happening *when* and *where,* for all activities, at all locations. Having local maps marked with routes is also a welcome idea. Figure 10.1 shows the Wing Family Centennial Reunion program, which describes five days of activities with a summary of costs and locations and a note that maps are available. (The Wood Reunion program had maps on the reverse side.)

Point the Way: Art Direction and Visual Effects

It's both helpful and decorative to have lots of signs around the reunion site to guide people to various activities. They can be prepared on poster board with colorful

WFA Centennial Reunion Program
June 13-16, 2002 -- East Sandwich, Massachusetts
Theme: Seeing Our Past -- Facing Our Future

Wednesday, June 12

6 p.m.   Pre-reunion early-bird get-together meal at Seafood Sam's*,
                Canal-side on Tupper Road, Sandwich

Thursday, June 13

10-4   Registration, refreshments, tours
                Wing Fort House, Spring Hill Road, East Sandwich
10-4   Quilters at the Fort House
6 p.m.   1640s Dinner (Grange Hall, $15)
                85 Old County Road, East Sandwich
                Seating limit: 75 Wear your 1640 duds

Friday, June 14

10-4   Registration, refreshments, tours at the Fort House
2 p.m.   WFA Board meeting (Sandwich Public Library)
10-4   Quilters at the Fort House
6 p.m.   Social hour - cash bar - Cape Codder Restaurant*
7 p.m.   Centennial Reunion Banquet ($30)
                Cape Codder Resort, 1225 Iyanough Road, Hyannis
                Program: "Meet Your Ancestors"

Saturday, June 15

9:30 a.m.   Annual WFA Business Meeting (all are welcome)
                Henry T. Wing School*, Route 130, Sandwich
11:30 a.m.   WFA Board meeting (Wing School)
12 noon   Picnic at the Fort House ($5)
                Steel folding chairs available - or bring your own lawn chairs
                (Rain location: Henry T. Wing School)
1:30 p.m.   WFA family photographs
2 p.m.   WFA benefit auction at the Fort House
6 p.m.   Social time - cash bar - Legion Pavilion*
6:30 p.m.   Roast pork buffet ($15)
                American Legion Pavilion, Route 130, Sandwich

Sunday, June 16

9 a.m.   Continental Breakfast at the Fort House (donation bucket)
10 a.m.   Centennial family worship at the Fort House
                Pres. Richard L. Wing, speaker; Choral music by The Cousins

A map of all activity locations will be available for viewing at the Fort House.

Figure 10.1 The Wing Family Centennial Reunion of 2002

markers or on a computer. Many computer inkjet printers allow use of prefolded banner paper, which then unfolds to display a sign of any length. Make sure you use large, readable lettering.

Check with hotel staff well beforehand about guidelines for placing signs inside. If no tape is permitted, ask if they can provide easels on which you can place signs attached to poster board or foam core. Outdoors, use removable tape to affix signs to structures, posts, or tables. (Of course, don't use nails on any property that does not belong to you.) If there are no surfaces on which to attach signs, consider using wooden stakes—like the type used for tomato plants, which you can get at a garden store. Then tack the signs onto the stake and insert it in soft grass near the site you wish to mark.

Here are some of the signs the Wood Reunion used, which are easily adaptable to your own circumstances.

- **Welcome! Please Sign In.** Two of these signs were made; one was placed just outside the door to the facility, and the other at the registration table.

- **Start Here to Meet Your Ancestors!** This marked the first of many wall charts placed around the room and on support columns in the room. These signs contained various genealogy charts of the descendants of the mutual ancestors. All attendees were guaranteed to find their individual names on at least one of the charts, which had been divided into color-coded lines from seven of the children of the mutual ancestors represented at the reunion.

- **Preserve the Past Here!** This sign directed people to the computer and scanner station, where a skilled volunteer scanned old photos and documents that had been brought to the reunion, as requested, for sharing. You'll learn more about the charts and scanned images in Chapter 11.

- **Group Photo Here at 2 P.M.** This sign was placed both inside and outside the door to the deck where the group was to assemble for the family photograph.

Additional signs posted included information about the free soft drinks and the cash bar for beer and wine, the location of the rest rooms, and the box in which to place evaluations at the end of the day.

Preserve Your Production on Film

As you view the historic photographs of the family from years gone by, they're a reminder that you can make the same gift to future generations by recording your reunion on film. While many family members will no doubt bring their own cameras, make sure you cover the event overall—without being limited to one family's views and choices. Whether you entrust one relative to the role of official photographer or videographer or your budget includes hiring a professional, you should prepare a list of events and scenes that you want recorded. These planned shots might include the arrival of some families, people at the registration desk, folks studying the charts and exhibits, games and contests, mealtimes, and special presentations. In your pre-reunion mailings, survey family members on their capabilities and willingness to serve as photographers.

Of course, some of the most beloved pictures are candid shots that were not planned at all. Those spontaneous moments can best be captured when a lot of cameras are in action, which you can accomplish quite inexpensively by purchasing a dozen disposable cameras to distribute to selected "assistant photographers." Sign out each camera to a specific person so you can make sure to collect them at the end of each day for processing. Figure 10.2 shows a sample camera label.

Volunteer Photographer 2
Catch our family having fun!
Return it here when you are done,
So we can share with everyone.

Figure 10.2 Label for disposable camera

It is easy today to have film developed in two formats at once—prints and digital, with the digital picture available either on a CD or through a Web site, depending on where you take the film for development. This way, you have permanent pictures for an album that can be copied for relatives who prefer that format, and you can e-mail digital copies anywhere in the world in a moment and upload them to a Web site. Announce several times during the reunion that while you are taking "official pictures," you would appreciate receiving copies of everyone else's photos and videos as well, so that they can be preserved in the archives for the next reunion—and the next century.

While some of the video cameras in use will pick up sound, having a small pocket tape recorder or two will add to your recording capabilities and enable you to record other family voices to add to the sound track. See Chapter 12 for a full discussion of oral and video interviews as part of your reunion.

Everyone Say "Cheese!"

I attended a reunion where our group of over one hundred people stood together in front of an ancestral barn while the photographer climbed up into a cherry-picker bucket mounted on a pickup truck—the kind used by utility workers and tree trimmers. As he was being raised to a height of about twenty feet above the crowd, each person was handed a 4 x 6 card with a unique number on it. The photographer asked us all to look up—holding the card under our chins with the number showing, while he snapped a few pictures. We were then asked to write our names clearly on the back of the card, without moving from our place, and a helper picked up all the cards. Then the photographer took the real photos. When the photos were developed, there was a clear record of the name of everyone in the picture from the trial shots with the numbers and every name was attributed to the correct person.

While a truck with a cherry-picker bucket has seemed an extreme expense at our other reunions, it is valuable to have a photographer positioned higher than the crowd. Once, we gathered outdoors near a lake and the photographer we hired mounted a stepladder to get the distance. Another time, the cameraman stood on the upper deck at the rear of the ski lodge while we gathered on a grassy spot below, looking up.

Some family groups pose for a commercial studio photographer. For a group shot of my extended family in 1998 (see Figure 10.3), the photographer asked each of us to wear simple dark clothing. Asking thirty people, including very young children, to sit for over an hour was quite a task—the little ones became very restless as time passed—but we were pleased to see the results of the photographer's vision, where each individual face is highlighted against the dark clothing. In fact, we remembered other group pictures taken on holidays when everyone's colorful clothing—the snowman sweaters, the Santa caps—competed for the viewer's attention and distracted from the faces of the individuals. From now on, we opt for dark clothing for professional group photographs.

At our 1994 Wood Family Reunion, the first in the extended family for over fifty years, one relative walked the grounds with a video camera interviewing people. We had not anticipated this, and our cousin had not planned a series of questions, so the interviews were uneven. (See Chapter 12 for more details.) But I will not soon forget

Figure 10.3 Wood family descendants in 1998

eighty-year-old Cousin Bob's smiling comment to the camera: "This is great, and we sure look forward to the next one." Sadly, Bob passed away before the next one, but we all cherish that video revealing his enthusiasm at meeting all the relatives for the first time since he was a young man.

Sound and Light Show

Depending on the type of production you stage, you have a range of lighting possibilities to consider, including color, spotlights, and strobe. Since lighting is important for both photography and videos, check all indoor facilities for their lighting capacity. Outdoors, you must rely on Mother Nature, so be concerned with the type of film being used—be sure that whether you find yourself in glaring sun or overcast shade, the exposure is just right.

Consider borrowing or leasing a big screen TV and VCR and inviting folks to bring along home videos of recent events—the latest wedding, a recent vacation, the previous reunion. Then run these family events continuously in a section of the hall, a separate room, or a tent.

Acoustics are equally important to your production planning. If the reunion is at a hotel or other full-service center, a sound system is likely installed and you can order a microphone through the leasing contract. Facilities at a park pavilion or community center location are less likely to have such a setup, so your team should determine what equipment is needed and how to obtain it. The sound director can be responsible for organizing this aspect.

We've found that the simplest microphone is a battery-operated bullhorn, which can be rented inexpensively. The one I own also plays brief excerpts from one hundred tunes at selectable volumes. You can be sure that when I turn on the bullhorn to play "Charge!" at full volume, everyone pays attention. And don't forget to purchase extra batteries.

Recorded music provides dimensions to the reunion experience and can create fun transitions between "acts" during the reunion. The sound director has lots of choices to make, depending on the venue. For indoor reunions, see whether a CD or tape player can be connected to the facility's sound system. Outdoors, a CD boom box or two will enliven the events. If a family member is a DJ and knows how to manage a full program of music, invite him or her in on the planning.

Costume Design

Having all reunion attendees wear T-shirts or caps made just for the get-together is a fun and easy way to warm up the crowd. These can be ordered from a variety of stores and Web sites (such as *family-reunion-t-shirts.com/index.html, www.internet-t-shirts.com/, www.getinprint.com, www.dftees.com,* and *www.marnexproducts.com),* but it's also fun to make your own. You can buy blank T-shirts at the nearest bargain store and have an artistic member of the team design a stencil to be painted on each shirt. Learn more about painting on fabric at *sewing.about.com/cs/fabricpaint/.*

I made special awards T-shirts for my reunion at home on my computer. All I needed were an inkjet color printer and transfer paper, which can be purchased at any major office supply store. Not a natural artist at all, I found an inexpensive software package that provided help with design and lettering. Once the transfer printed out, I affixed it to each shirt with a hot iron. You can find free software online at *www.hanes2u.com,* or you can purchase commercial software from *www.novadevelopment.com/Store/Print.aspx.*

Figure 10.4 Children serving as color guard for a cemetery ceremony

Figure 10.5 Chairman of the Souther Reunion publicizing the Hawaii site

Almost anything can be imprinted—including your reunion logo. Only your budget will limit the number and kind of items you personalize for reunion participants. Some reunions request orders in advance and prepayments for T-shirts, which works well if you have someone dedicated to all the record keeping and paperwork. You can also order a batch of mixed sizes and give or sell them at the reunion.

T-shirts aren't the only way to dress up a reunion. For a special grave-marking ceremony at our last reunion, we were unable to secure the services of a military color guard, so I created a color guard composed of my two grandsons, then ages eight and ten (see Figure 10.4). I found two colonial three-cornered hats at a party store and clad one boy in a bright red T-shirt and the other in bright blue. One carried in the American flag, followed by the second, while my son, who is a professional singer, provided a rousing rendition of "The Star Spangled Banner."

You might also consider local customs for your costume ideas. As you see in Figure 10.5, Richard Souther encourages participants to consider local dress for the 2005 family reunion in Hawaii. Relatives who don't bring Hawaiian clothing with them can no doubt obtain these items once they arrive. The typical souvenir leis and other garb are certain to become meaningful mementos when all the rolls of film are developed.

Parade of the Ancestors

At the Wing Family Centennial Reunion, a procession of costumed family members representing key members of the original immigrant family was a thrilling event and a great way to connect with families of centuries past. Other reunions have created brief skits in which a moment in the history of their families is reenacted. These "family plays" can be as simple or elaborate as time and talents permit—from a simple parade to a full-blown production with songs and dances. All that is required is a family genealogist or historian to write a sketch that briefly tells the story about who the first settlers were, where they landed, and when. The Web offers wonderful research resources at such sites as *memory.loc.gov/*, the American Memory Collection of the Library of Congress. With actors dressed in period costumes rented or sewn by family members, you can be sure the cameras will be clicking away.

Living History

Figure 10.6 Historical presentation by Mark Lowe

If no one in your family is stagestruck, consider reenactors or living history enthusiasts, who have developed costumed presentations of historic personalities and might perform your family's story for you.

My friend Mark Lowe has combined genealogy and family history in a unique way. To promote a public awareness project for historic cemeteries, he inspired members of both the Southern Kentucky Genealogical Society and the Robertson County (Tennessee) Historical Society to join in developing costumed presentations of several people buried in historic cemeteries. This evolved into fund-raisers known as "Afternoon at Pioneer Cemetery" and "Evening at Elmwood," in which guests enjoy an elegant box lunch or supper followed by a walking tour of the historic grave sites. During the tour, costumed interpreters present the stories of individuals buried there (see Figure 10.6).

The presenters have done considerable historical and genealogical research on their characters, using public records, diaries, letters, and other information. They have carefully studied period costumes to create a presentation that is both historically accurate and entertaining. With this preparation and scripts created to reflect the characters' own life experiences, the presenters seem to become the person they represent.

Mark relates that on one occasion, after a presentation as a nineteenth century gentleman named Mr. Barclay, he was approached by a visitor who was a Barclay descendant. She'd heard stories about her ancestor from her grandmother, and was moved to tell Mark, "You are just like Granny Max said you were!" Because that event was captured on videotape, it is still shown and enjoyed at Barclay family reunions.

You'll find more information about costumed presentations and reenactments at *www.alhfam.org* and *www.youcanlivehistory.com.*

You've now set the stage for your big reunion production, and we're ready to move on to Chapter 11, where you decide what to offer that will amuse, entertain, inform, and delight your family members.

CHAPTER **11**

The Lobby Showcase

As in the theater lobby of a Broadway show, where there is often a collection of displays, souvenirs for sale, and other enticements to entertain the patrons, your team should create a showcase of exhibits—maps, photographs, heirlooms, artifacts, and more.

Look Who's Here!

Ever since use of the camera became commonplace in the late nineteenth century, families have collected images—even families of the most modest means splurged on a photograph once in a while. My widowed paternal grandmother arrived in the United States from Canada in 1912 with the youngest of her children to join older ones already living and working in Boston. They lived on the top floor of a wooden three-family tenement house in an immigrant section of the city. Three members, including Grandmother, died during the influenza epidemic of 1918. The five surviving children, then aged fifteen and up, including one son serving in the Army during World War I, kept a family home together into the 1930s. Few photographs remain, but those that do are precious.

One is a formal portrait of my father at age eleven, taken two years after his arrival in the United States, proudly dressed in a school uniform (see Figure 11.1). The other is a simple snapshot of Grandmother and an aunt that was taken on the fire escape of the tenement building. Both women perished in 1918—this is the only known image

Figure 11.1 My father around 1914

of two family members the present generation never knew. We also have a wonderful 1859 photograph (see Figure 11.2) of Joseph Wood Jr., my maternal great-great-great-grandfather, celebrating his hundredth birthday, the first centenarian in the town of Lebanon, New Hampshire. We descendants all hope we have inherited some of his longevity genes.

These are the types of photographs that are perfect to bring to a reunion. They trigger wonderful memories and story telling: "Remember this?" "My, he certainly had the family chin." In one of your mailings, request that participants bring along photos and photo albums as carefully labeled as possible. But don't be surprised if most are not. One of the common curses of albums and old photographs is that rarely are all of the persons in the picture identified by name. We have a photo taken of a Wood family reunion in 1911 (see Figure 11.3), which I took to the 1994 reunion in hopes of identifying everyone. Few of those in the photo were still living, but many of their children were in attendance. By the end of the day, we were able to put a name to every face.

At one reunion, I found the only known photo of me at age two wearing my cowboy boots. This had special meaning because when my grandmother was terminally ill, she asked my grandfather to use her World War II ration stamps to buy me—their only grandchild—a pair of cowboy boots. My oldest child later wore those boots, and I still have them.

—Barbara Brixey Wylie

Figure 11.2 Joseph Wood Jr. on his one hundredth birthday in November 1859

Photo historian and genealogist Maureen A. Taylor, author of *Preserving Your Family Photographs* (Cincinnati: Betterway Books, 2001) and *Uncovering Your Ancestry Through Family Photographs* (Cincinnati: Betterway Books, 2000), writes: "A family photograph collection is more than a random collection of images; it is a time capsule of the lives of our ancestors." If you have old photos without the slightest clue about the identity of the people in them, go to the online service at *www.familytreemagazine.com/photos*, which helps identify people in old family photographs.

Figure 11.3 Wood family reunion in July 1911

Secrets of the Scanner

Many folks are likely to ask for copies of some of the old photos in your showcase; you can give them instant satisfaction if you have a laptop and a scanner with you. When you survey the family for their computer skills and equipment, look for someone who not only has the equipment, but also knows how to use it. Then set up a special table at the reunion for scanning.

Figure 11.4 Five generations of the Hartman family in 1913

Scanners are perfectly safe and will not inflict any damage on old photos. (In fact, once the pictures are digitized, a skilled operator is able to actually restore old damage such as cracks and discoloration.) Figure 11.4 shows a 1913 photograph that includes five generations of the Hartman family, the oldest having been born in 1823. It was digitized and sent to me via e-mail attachment.

Putting Your Family on the Map

Reunions bring to one location family members from all over the map—so why not mount a map? It's a visual reminder of the family's settlements across the country, or perhaps even in other countries. Beyond the map, though, you can find other ways to highlight the different parts of the world in which your family members currently live:

- Collecting regional recipes for a family cookbook
- Organizing regional dishes for the reunion potluck dinner
- Offering presentations by groups on their home communities
- Rotating the reunion site among various family hometowns

Bobbi King conducts bus tours of the Hytrek family's ancestors' lands. She has also displayed copies of land patents filed by ancestors; such copies are available from the National Archives.

> *I have a large U.S. map, where I show the migration patterns of the four immigrant ancestors, beginning at their arrival point of New York. Colored pushpins, a specific color for each ancestor family, trace the settlement of the Hytrek families. I string a piece of colored yarn to trace the migration and settlement of each ancestor, and then fasten colored pushpins where their descendants settled across the United States.*
>
> —Bobbi King

Heirlooms and Artifacts

What makes something an "heirloom"? Its age? Its monetary value? Actually, neither. Any piece of personal property passed on, through law or gift, from an inheritance is considered an heirloom. It may have little or large financial value, and it may be cherished or discarded by future generations.

My sister once had an antique shop with many items that came from estate sales. Old, small, framed photographs and portraits; jewelry; inscribed silverware; and similar items that had obviously once been cherished family possessions were now "orphaned" and sold to strangers. Occasionally, we found a clue as to ownership—an inscription on the back or the name of a portrait studio and city. We used these clues to try to locate any living descendants so we could return the property to the family. In fact, the Web site *www.petuniapress.com* publishes a free online newsletter called *Somebody's Links,* listing heirlooms and artifacts found by persons seeking family owners. Two typical items from the newsletter are reproduced in Figures 11.5 and 11.6.

```
While shopping in an antique store in Fredonia, Chautauqua County,
New York on Saturday, 31 August 2002, I found two wonderful Bibles
which had belonged to the DUTTON family. The genealogical
information is extensive, extending from 1792 in New York and New
England at least through the 1960s in Arizona... In addition,
there is a beautiful Marriage Certificate complete with a Revenue
Stamp.

Previously published in SOMEBODY'S LINKS NEWSLETTER: Genealogical
Treasures Found, Vol. 4, No. 31, 3 September 2002.
http://www.PetuniaPress.com/
```

Figure 11.5 Heirlooms in search of a family

```
I have 17 unidentified cabinet photographs from my grandmother's
album. Most of these were made in various studios in Mt. Vernon,
Jefferson County, Illinois and probably date from the late 1800s.
They are possibly of WILSON, OSBORN, and CARPENTER families, and
perhaps of persons who married family members. Among these would
be VAUGHN, MANNION, and HAWKER. There are also six tintypes. I
would be glad to send scans of any or all to those researching
anyone with one of these surnames who was in the area during that
time period, in return for help in identifying the subjects.

Previously published in SOMEBODY'S LINKS NEWSLETTER: Genealogical
Treasures Found, Vol. 4, No. 31, 3 September 2002.
http://www.PetuniaPress.com/
```

Figure 11.6 Ancestors in search of families

Whether your family heirlooms are old letters, ledger books, a marriage certificate, an ancient passport, a silver spoon, a hand-turned wooden bowl, furniture, or clothing, each piece of personal property handed down to the present day has a story to tell. Do you know the story that goes with your heirlooms? Do your family members? The rest of the family would be thrilled to hear about them, which is why displaying them at the reunion will be so much fun.

Don't ask people to bring priceless items that belong in a bank vault; instead, they can bring photos of those. Try to include a small written paragraph about each piece you display, and have a volunteer standing by to answer questions or refer inquiries to the present owner.

I wear one particular heirloom to all the Wood reunions; the rest of the time it remains in a locked safe. In the summer of 1869, my maternal great-grandparents, Jeremiah and Martha Ellen (Dickinson) Wood, lost three small children to diphtheria in one month. As was the custom of the day, strands of the children's hair were gently woven together and then placed into a golden locket as a memorial. Martha wore that locket in every formal photograph for the rest of her life, and I am now its steward during my lifetime. I wear the locket to family reunions and share the story of this sad event in our family's history, so that we may all honor our ancestors—and through this heirloom remember their tragedies as well as their triumphs.

How is an "artifact" different from an heirloom? An artifact is any product of human workmanship that has archaeological or historical interest; artifacts are perfect items to display at a reunion showcase. Our 1999 Wood Reunion was honored with a gift of "golden spikes" from a railroad that had played an important role in the family's history (see the story on page 148).

For Wood Family Reunion showcases, I often assemble a large collection of photographs and copies of original documents in large three-ring binders. I label the albums Treasure Book 1, Treasure Book 2, and so on, and place them on the Treasure Table. Other family members contribute maps, vintage clothing items, and old farm and kitchen tools that have been in the family for generations. We all enjoy a fascinating history lesson by visiting the Treasure Table and hearing the stories of the past, envisioning our ancestors as real people.

Finding Yourself on Genealogy Wall Charts

A major feature of any reunion is providing an opportunity to visualize the relationships of one family group to another. Perhaps your family has a resident historian who has recorded family information and can create charts depicting those relationships. If not, now is the time to encourage a family member to explore the fascinating study of genealogy—or to hire a genealogist to do the work for you.

To find a reliable family researcher in your community, start with the local genealogical or historical society or large public library, which may have a list of reputable genealogists. Many such repositories have copies of membership directories published by the Board for Certification of Genealogists (BCG) and the Association of Professional Genealogists (APG). Both organizations publish their directories on the Web. At *www.bcgcertification.org* and *www.apgen.org,* you can search by locality and specialty to find a genealogist who can assist you personally or recommend someone to you.

In 2001 I served as the project genealogist for an event designed to discover living descendants of eighty-three men who served as lighthouse keepers at Cape Hatteras, North Carolina, from 1803 to 1939. We planned a major reunion, the Hatteras

The Northern Railroad Golden Spikes

The Northern Railroad figured prominently in the lives of the Wood family of Lebanon, New Hampshire. First approved in 1844, the railroad opened from Concord to Lebanon in 1847 and extended to West Lebanon in 1848. It brought profits to many family members, who sold land to the railroad, and provided accommodations for the workers. In 1852 alone, over seventy-six thousand passengers traveled on the popular Northern.

The Wood Family Reunion memory book includes recollections of Josie Ellen Wood, youngest daughter of Jeremiah. In addition to his own shares, Jeremiah purchased a share of railroad stock for each of his fourteen children, which entitled them to an annual shareholders' adventure on the train from West Lebanon to the big city of Concord. Josie never forgot those wonderful childhood trips.

After World War II, with the development of the Federal Interstate Highway system, the railroads lost most passenger business and faced financial problems, forcing smaller lines to close. Passenger service on the Northern ended in 1964, with the last freight train moving through in 1991. The New Hampshire Department of Transportation obtained ownership of the lines, and the railroad removed its track by 1995. The land corridor of rail lines was then designated for the Rails to Trails program, converting the scenic pathway for public recreational use.

To create the Northern Rail Trail, a fifty-nine-mile run from Boscawen to Lebanon, 140,000 railroad ties were removed. The trail now includes a two-mile waterfront section along Lake Mascoma and provides a recreational trail for hikers, bikers, and snowmobilers in season.

Cousin Roger Wood obtained many of the original railroad spikes that were removed from the tracks and graciously donated them as special gifts at our 1999 reunion. Each colorful artifact (the "gold" was added recently) honors our own Wood family's history in Lebanon. Many of these spikes are now over 150 years old. They are treasures from our family's past.

Keepers Descendants Homecoming, to honor those brave keepers and their kin by sharing their experiences and the history of the lighthouse, which had recently been safely moved back from the eroding edge of the sea.

In a solid year of research, I found over 10,200 names to place in my computerized database and charted generation by generation through public records, family memories, primary documents, Civil War pensions, and other sources. Over twelve hundred descendants registered to attend the event, traveling to North Carolina's Outer Banks from as far away as Hawaii, including many family groups whose children had never been to North Carolina before. Now that was a big reunion!

My goal was to include every registered person on a chart showing their place on the family tree. Because the Outer Banks is rural, early families had often intermarried with one another; thus many living people were direct descendants of several lighthouse keepers, and their names appeared on several charts. It was quite an undertaking, but totally worthwhile.

The size of a chart can depend on both the number of descendants and the format selected for the display. Elissa Scalise Powell prepared a wall chart for her Hartman family reunion that was too big to hang up indoors—it took several helpers to attach her 2-by-42-foot chart to the side of the house!

You can download free charts from *www.pbs.org/kbyu/ancestors/charts* and *www.genealogysearch.org/free/forms.html,* then fill in your family's information by hand. Or develop a computerized family database with one of the many genealogy software programs available, and print charts from the database. For genealogy software, go to Cyndi's List *(www.cyndislist.com/software.htm);* while you're there, look around. You'll find tutorials, support, and other tools to help you automate your family records.

Although you can print charts from a genealogy program on a regular computer printer, a lengthy line involves much matching and taping together of many printed sheets. I often use the services of a commercial chart-printing service—

For more information on genealogy software programs, see another book in the NGS series: *Genealogy 101: How to Trace Your Family's History and Heritage* by Barbara Renick.

www.chartform.com—and am then able to transmit the information by e-mail attachment. The charts arrive in a few weeks, rolled in mailing tubes. Some have been over twenty feet long and required much help and imagination to display.

For our smaller Wood family reunions, we have been tracking the descendants of nine children of one couple. To date, descendants from seven of these lines have been found, and research continues as we determine whether the other two have any living family members. At the display, a color-coding system directs people to the appropriate charts. Each of the seven lines has a separate color at the top of the chart. These charts use the "descendant box" format, which is easy to view and understand. Figure 11.7 shows one of our charts, which depicts just the first three generations, left to right. Additional charts took each grandchild down to the present day.

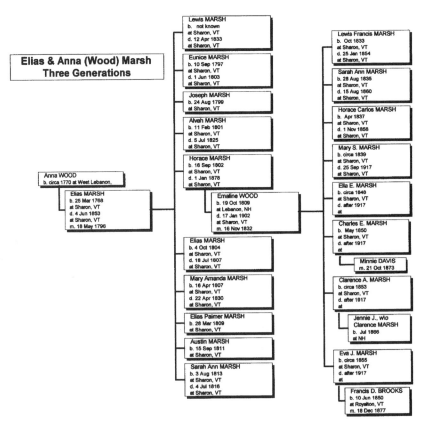

Figure 11.7 Genealogy box chart—three generations

Ye Olde Reunion Shoppe

Back in Chapter 4, we discussed various fund-raising possibilities for the reunion: bake sales, flea markets, family auctions, memento sales. The showcase can also display selected items for sale as souvenirs or raffle prizes. A production team member should be stationed at this location to assist visitors, register sales, and keep records.

Small Souvenirs

A nice touch is to include some small souvenirs or mementos for everyone, as part of the registration fee. The memento can go into the goodie bags distributed at registration. (Chapter 14 details the registration process.) But items like T-shirts and caps are good candidates to sell in the Reunion Shoppe at the showcase. Draw attention to the T-shirt by placing one shirt on a hanger, suspended from a nearby hook, or stuff one with straw or cotton as you might a scarecrow on Halloween. Clearly post the prices and sizes available; prices should reflect not only the basic cost, but also any taxes and shipping costs. Other items that sell well include baseball caps, sun visors, ballpoint pens, and computer mouse pads. *Www.logos2promos.com* advertises over half a million items for your Reunion Shoppe, and you can search for more by going to any Web search engine, such as Google or Yahoo, and typing *personalized gifts +reunion.* Just be sure to place orders well in advance so there is no chance of empty space at your Reunion Shoppe.

Raffles and Door Prizes

Make sure everyone is eligible for some extra prizes—perhaps door prizes announced when your large group gathers. There is no charge for door prizes. For these drawings, add a unique number to the front or back of the nametag. Then at drawing time, all you need is a basket in which all of those numbers are placed. That way, there's no need for individual prize tickets.

Raffles can raise money, and one of the best prizes is a handmade quilt. If your family group is missing quilt makers in this generation, you can find help online. Go to *www.threadsunlimited.com/monotree.html* and *www.familytreequilts.com* for ideas and resources on having these treasures made and personalized to offer as a prized raffle item at your reunion.

Other items might well produce extra reunion income and be raffled off. Ask the family craftspersons to suggest handmade donations. Send the team out to solicit larger gifts from area merchants. Place all the items to be raffled off in one section of your showcase. Get just one double roll of tickets to sell at whatever price range suits you—two dollars each or six for ten dollars. When the raffle is held, the winning ticket entitles that lucky person to select the prize he wants from the raffle table. Early winners get to pick from the whole collection.

The Special American Flag

An unusual raffle or door prize is a very special American flag. Every day of the year, staff members carry boxes of American flags to a roof of the U.S. Capitol. One by one, they are unfolded, quickly raised and lowered, and returned to another box. One of the best kept secrets about benefits available to you as an American citizen is that you can own a flag flown over the U.S. Capitol in your honor or in honor of an event. You can request that your flag be flown on a certain date, and if you mention in your letter that the date is for the family reunion, this information will be included on the certificate of authenticity issued by the Office of the Architect of the Capitol that accompanies the flag on delivery.

Caution: Commercial Web sites promise to get you a flag flown over the Capitol for fifty dollars or more. Ignore them! These unnecessary intermediaries are deviously seeking to cash in on something you can purchase yourself for far less. Instead, work directly with the office of your own member of Congress for prices in the seventeen-to-thirty-dollar range, including shipping, depending on the size and material you select.

You can choose your fabric—cotton or nylon—and the size you desire. All of these flags are made in the United States. Order and purchase the flag through the office of your U.S. senator or representative. The price is modest, but the specific price actually varies slightly from one congressional office to another. Since each member of Congress has an individual Web site, look there for details. To find the names and addresses and Web sites for your senators or representative on the Web, just click *www.senate.gov* and *www.house.gov* for the current contact information. Place your

Win A Very Special American Flag!

Through the assistance of the offices of U.S. Senator Robert Smith (R, NH), we have a very special grand prize.

A 3'x5' American flag was raised and flown over the U.S. Capitol in Washington, D.C., this morning, July 31, 1999, to honor our gathering. A certificate will be inscribed with the date, and that it was flown to commemorate the Wood Family Reunion, Descendants of Joseph and Anna (Palmer) Wood.

This flag and certificate of commemoration will be shipped within thirty days to the winner of the raffle grand prize today! Then on each holiday in the future, the winning family can proudly display this flag for which the Wood family fought and served since 1775.

Figure 11.8 The American flag door prize

order a few months before the reunion; arrival takes four to eight weeks. And be sure to advertise the flag in your promotional and publicity materials (see Figure 11.8).

Now we're ready to move on to the final arrangements for the big opening night of your family reunion production. The magical moment is almost here.

Act 3
Getting the Show on the Road

CHAPTER 12

Interviewing the Stars

Oral Histories

FAMILY HISTORY INVOLVES GATHERING BOTH PAPER DOCUMENTS AND oral reminiscences. The cherished pages of my grandmother's childhood memories were created when one of her daughters sat down with her for that special purpose, engaged her in a guided conversation, and wrote down her recollections. I was just a teenager when this took place, and it had absolutely no meaning to me at that time. After all, I still visited with my grandmother often and heard her tell all kinds of stories. Now, half a century later, with both my aunt and grandmother having long ago joined their ancestors, my perceptions have certainly changed.

Conducting an oral interview is a simple process, requiring just a pad of paper, note cards, pen or pencil, clipboard, batteries, and a small tape recorder. If you decide to conduct some oral interviews at the reunion, make a list of those senior family members who are candidates for interviews and consider which relatives would most likely facilitate a meaningful interview with each of them.

Preparing for the Interviews

If possible, contact the people you want interviewed *before* the reunion and let them know of the family's special interest in their life's experiences. Recruit the interviewers before the reunion as well, so you can explain the process and the ways you hope they can enjoy the experience. To save time, during pre-reunion visits to the facility

What a delicious feeling I had when I sneaked into the forbidden parlor! The musty odor was incense to me. To handle the photograph album and the large seashells— to put the same shells to my ear and hear the sea roar, to sit on the hair-cloth sofa on a hot day, and to softly touch the keys of the old spinet were my secret joys.

—Josie Wood Wardrobe (my grandmother), interviewed in the 1950s, recalling her childhood in the 1880s

or site, try to pinpoint where the interview can occur—a quiet place away from noise and distractions.

So that there is some consistency to the interviews, your team should develop a series of questions before the reunion and write or print them on cards or sheets of paper, with lots of space in between for the answers.

Ask Open-ended Questions

To encourage sharing, word your questions carefully. Consider the differences in these three pairs of questions:

1a. What is your name?

1b. Do you know how you got your name? Were you named for someone else? Did you have a nickname when you were growing up? What was it? Do you know how you got that nickname? How did you feel about it when you were called that?

2a. What is your birthplace?

2b. When you were a small child, where did you live and what did your house look like?

3a. Did you like school?

3b. Please think about a day in grade school that you remember—what was going on? Who was there? What happened?

The first question in each pair is limiting; it basically asks for a one-word answer. The second question in each pair seeks the same information, but is worded in a way that encourages the interviewee to remember things about the past that will add substance and texture to the interview.

Interviewing older persons requires patience and flexibility. They may wander off the topic or specific question, so just listen for a while, as you may learn some additional details that enrich the experience. Then gently guide the person's attention back to your clipboard with questions. Do not interrupt the storyteller or correct any statements—besides being rude, interrupting can cause the person to lose the train of thought.

Good opening lines are "Tell me about . . ." or "What do you remember about . . . ?" Ask about the oldest family member this person ever met as a child. This may take you

Veterans History Project

Do you have a military veteran in your family or neighborhood? The Library of Congress and its American Folklife Center need your help in collecting and preserving oral histories from our nation's veterans. By "veterans," they mean all men and women who served in any war (World War I, World War II, and the Korean, Vietnam, and Persian Gulf wars) or in any branch of military service, as well as those who served on the home front as civilians engaged in activities that supported the armed services.

The project will create a national collection of personal histories on audiotape and videotape, as well as letters, diaries, maps, photographs, and home movies. These items will be of lasting value to future historians, educators, students, authors, filmmakers, and family members.

I have volunteered for this project, even though I have no immediate living family members who are military veterans, because I believe it is important to create a lasting legacy of recorded interviews and other documents. I have a friend who served as a nurse in Vietnam and have made plans to interview her.

The Veterans History Project has a Web site at *www.loc.gov/folklife/vets*, where you can find detailed information on recording a veteran's oral history, including sample interview questions, forms, and technical tips to help interviewers be more effective in the interview and recording process.

back several more generations with stories the rest of the family has never heard before. Old photographs are a good way to trigger memories: "What can you tell me about this picture?" If you need to clarify a statement, wait for a pause, then ask, "Let me understand that story about the summertime work in the fields. Do you mean that all the children in the family helped out gathering the berries and vegetables, or just you?"

Try not to press for answers. If the interviewee seems uncomfortable, ask, "Would you rather talk about something else?" and shift the conversation to another topic. If you ask "When?" and the response is "I don't know," try another approach. "About how old were you when . . . ?" or "Did this happen before or after you were married?" can help organize memories of long ago.

If you select several senior family members to be interviewed, plan to have a few common questions asked of each one: "What's the most important event that has happened in your lifetime?" or "What advice would you want to give to future generations?" These similar responses can then be grouped together to serve another purpose—perhaps a section of the next reunion's memory book called "Wisdom from the Past" could include each person's name, age, and response. As a group, the responses will provide memorable reading.

Mini-Interviews at the Reunion

If time for long interviews is not available, you can still conduct brief interviews, as a team of "roving reporters" circulates among the family. Since each reporter might not have an individual tape recorder, print questions on large 5 x 8 file cards so answers can be written right on the card.

The mini-interviews could well lead to a longer, follow-up visit after the reunion. Find out if the person who conducted the brief interview would be willing to expand it sometime in the near future. The sooner you can do an expanded interview, the better, as the questions will be "fresh" in the minds of the reporter and the subject, and that will likely result in a more productive follow-up interview.

During the general sharing time, ask each reporter to come forward and share the question and answer he or she found most interesting during the interviews. You can also turn the event into a quiz game by having the reporter read the question and answer *without* first naming the person involved and then asking the audience to guess the identity of the "star" who was interviewed.

The time to interview older members of the family is now. The reunion of lighthouse keepers' descendants described in the previous chapter had been a long-held dream of one of the local residents, who had grown up in the lighthouse where his father had been a keeper. Years went by, and the event remained just a dream. The thought "Wouldn't it be nice if we could . . . " had not become an active plan. That man was nearing eighty when a severe stroke left him unable to walk or talk. While his mind remained bright, he could no longer tell the stories of lighthouse life that others enjoyed hearing. But as he sat in his wheelchair in the homecoming tent surrounded by twelve hundred keeper kin, his delight was apparent. Still, how we all wished he could have shared some of those stories once more. He passed away a few months later.

Preserving the Oral Interviews

Your planning should include managing a post-reunion project, where volunteers transcribe the oral history tapes and preserve them on paper and in a computerized file. Place copies, along with a photograph of the interviewee, with the family historian for long-term preservation. You might also plan on displaying a collection of them for the next reunion.

These are the voices of the past to save for the future. Make backup tapes right away, and store the originals in a safe place. Allowing for technology transfer in the decades ahead, these voices can be heard one hundred years from now by people who never had the opportunity to know their ancestors personally.

Publish a Book

For the 2001 Hatteras Keepers Descendants Homecoming, we gathered oral histories and genealogical research on the families of the lighthouse keepers. Family members donated historic photographs and other documents to add to those copied from public records. *Hatteras Keepers: Oral and Family Histories* was the result (see Figure 12.1), published by the Outer Banks Lighthouse Society, and a copy was given to each family attending the homecoming event. Many families learned for the first time of all the history, relationships, and significant heritage they shared. The book was then placed on public sale, where it enjoyed continuing attention. (For more details about this project, go to *www.outer-banks.com/hatteraskeepers/*.)

You too can consider self-publishing a collection of family stories and histories. Gather up the old photographs to be scanned, the stories from the oral interviews, old newspaper clippings about family events, and combine them with family history charts to produce your own limited-edition book. Chapter 13 details my experience creating

Figure 12.1 Compiling oral interviews into a commemorative book

and self-publishing smaller memory books for my family reunions. And *www.cyndis-list.com/oral.htm* offers other references for writing and publishing family stories.

Filming the Folks

Adding a camera (and camera operator) to the oral history interview can produce a wonderful, lasting visual and audio treat. A team needs to practice together before the reunion to be sure the video camera is unobtrusive and will not distract the participants. It's also important that the cameraperson pan the camera back and forth between the interviewer and the interviewee, as well as take shots of the larger scene around them at the time, while the microphone picks up the entire conversation. These video moments can be edited after the reunion to add to other filming done that day.

Learn how to create your own family documentary at *www.giftofheritage.com.* You can find more online information on how to edit videos and add titles, graphics, and special effects at *desktopvideo.miningco.com/cs/editit* and *www.videoguys.com/dtvhome.html.*

Permissions

While formal consent forms might be intimidating to the interviewee, they are still a good idea, given concerns for privacy. So do confirm in writing that the interviewee gives you permission to share the interview with others. You can adapt the sample form in Figure 12.2 to your own needs. To ease anyone's concerns, you might also promise to personally review the interview results with the interviewee before using it in any way in the future. And then ask if you may include it in reunion materials. Whether you share the interview informally from the microphone during the reunion, write it down for inclusion in the family's memory books, or upload it to a family Web site, your responsibility is to be honest, discreet, and tactful in reporting.

Permission to Interview

I give my permission to _____ to tape this

   interview with me for the purpose of recording our family history.

Signed_____ Date_____

Figure 12.2 Permission form for oral interviews

Common Sense and Confidentiality

Suppose Great-uncle Willie whispers, "You wanna know the real reason my Aunt Belle left home? She ran off with the preacher and had a baby." Do not accept every word as an accurate and long-unknown family secret! It may be a true story—or a nasty rumor. Others may have heard it before and think it's true, but have no evidence to support that claim. In any case, there is little value—and lots of potential consequences—to your retelling a potentially scandalous story right now.

Be very careful that what you retain and preserve from the interview will in no way seriously embarrass, offend, or cause personal distress or harm to any person who is being interviewed or to any person living or dead who was discussed during the interview. I heard a story similar to Uncle Willie's about a member of my family, recorded it, and placed it in a secure and controlled area of my computer genealogy program that does not print out in any reports. I have decided that after the deaths of all members of the generation in which the incident allegedly happened, I might again try to research the event in public records to confirm or deny its existence.

Everyone's a Star

In addition to one-on-one interviews, you can also shine the spotlight on a panel of relatives sitting at a table to share stories with the gathered group. Those who shared

> We children all went barefoot until we were twelve or thirteen years old. Even then, I remember being sent to school with shoes on and—when I was out of sight of home—taking off my shoes, hiding them in the bushes, and ferreting them out on the way home. On the days we wore them all the way to school, we would put them under our desks. Then when company came in, we would hustle them on . . . . At that time, women were beginning to wear bustles. One day, we girls all walked in from recess with our hats, coats—anything we could find—tucked under the back of our dress for a bustle. Of course, it brought our skirts above our knees in back. There was an uproar from the boys, and we went out in disgrace.
>
> — Josie Wood Wardrobe (my grandmother), interviewed in the 1950s, recollecting her childhood in the 1880s

a particular time in history—growing up during World War II, for example—have many memories that can be awakened when others are discussing the same events. At the Hatteras Homecoming, a panel of seniors shared their recollections of childhood in that rural seacoast community. The children in the audience were especially fascinated to hear about a time when there were no paved roads or buses, and people visited other communities by boat or by letting the air out of a car's tires and driving it up the hard sand at low tide.

You can find resources for writing your own life story at *www.turningmemories.com*, where you can order books or download e-books on the topic. The PBS video series *Ancestors* has a Web site at *broadcasting.byu.edu/ancestors/records/familyhistory*, where you can learn more about how to organize, write, and publish your family history.

Is your family one that immigrated to the United States in more recent generations? Are there memories remaining about that special time? My father and his siblings all grew up on a lakeside farm in rural Canada before moving to Boston as children in the early twentieth century. I heard many stories about what life was like there and then, but no one ever wrote it down. Today I wish that we had more of those memories on record. In recent years, I visited Canada to learn about the family's history and met a second cousin who had pictures and stories to share. You can be sure I wrote everything down!

The oral interviews shouldn't focus only on the senior members of the family—they aren't the only ones with stories to tell. Look for other relatives with unique experiences who would be willing to share them. How about Cousin Larry's adventures as a mountain climber? Or Aunt Dorothy's prized collection of English bone china? While their immediate family groups may know about these interests, the larger gathering may never have learned about them before.

The "stars" of your production are the family members who attend, and planning ahead for oral and filmed interviews will ensure that you have a permanent record of the wonderful event. It may be the first time or the last time you will have these very same people together, and it's a once-in-a-lifetime opportunity to preserve the memories. In the next chapter, we will explore some other ways to preserve family memories and honor your family's heritage.

CHAPTER **13**

Honoring the Family's Past

MUCH OF THE FUN AT A FAMILY REUNION SURROUNDS THE GROUPS gathered to chat, eat together, sing, play, enjoy one another's company, and otherwise celebrate. But underlying all the high-spirited activities is a sincere and serious responsibility to mark and measure the meaning of the day in terms of honoring this legacy that has been given to the living by those who came before.

Memorials and Tributes

There are many ways to honor the family ancestors during your family reunions. Learning more about their lives, sharing information among all branches of the family, holding special services at the ancestral church or synagogue—all help to raise your awareness and appreciation of this legacy.

Visit the Old Family Church

Perhaps you can still visit the church or meetinghouse that was at the center of your ancestors' lives in their original hometown. The West Lebanon Congregational Church was founded by many of the Wood family ancestors in the 1850s and stands today, a vital part of the community. At our 1994 reunion, we arranged with the minister of the church to attend the Sunday morning service as a group. I prepared a small insert for the church bulletin about our family's role in the church's history, including excerpts from two published sermons by ancestral Wood clergy.

The reunion was held at the end of July, when many local families were on vacation, so there was no worry about our overcrowding the small church. We were ushered to the front pews, and the minister acknowledged our presence in his remarks. The children in our family group, especially, were visibly moved by the significance of the event—all remained quiet and attentive. After the service, we joined the parishioners in the parish hall for coffee and conversation.

Old Family Burying Ground

Growing up in the small historic town of Lexington, Massachusetts, I was raised with history in the air. On each Memorial Day, I joined other children dressed in their Sunday best and carried new small American flags to place at the grave sites of the veterans buried in the oldest cemeteries. In many cases, these were veterans of the American Revolution, which had its first skirmish there on the Lexington village green in 1775. We learned at an early age to respect and honor those who had lived and died to build and protect America. As part of its family reunion weekend in Kentucky, the Vardiman family honored its heritage with a cemetery rededication service after its ancestral cemetery had been relocated (see Figure 13.1).

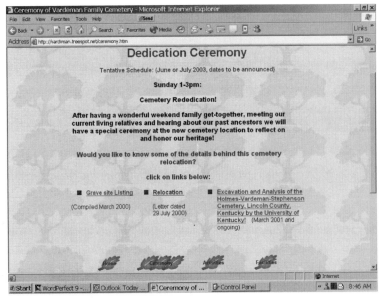

Figure 13.1 Announcement for Vardiman family cemetery rededication

Restore the Cemetery

Many old cemeteries are in a sad state of neglect—small family plots in rural areas have become overgrown with roots and brush, and headstones have been toppled by trees, buried by vines, worn by erosion, or defaced by vandals. The Meacham family decided to do something about it. Finding two old family cemeteries in Kentucky that had been abandoned and neglected, they arranged a restoration project. First, they contacted the current landowners, who graciously consented to the plan and provided access to the property for anyone with ancestors buried in the two cemeteries. The family located and retained a gravestone restorer, and after three days of heavy work—which included tree cutting and gravestone repair—the cemeteries were restored at a cost of about six hundred dollars per cemetery. The results were remarkable. You can read more about this project at *freepages.genealogy.rootsweb.com/~wmeacham/cemrest.htm* and view the pictures of its progress. It may inspire your family to do something similar.

The Association for Gravestone Studies at *www.gravestonestudies.org* provides helpful pointers about "Gravestone Rubbing Do's and Don'ts" and "Tools and Materials for Gravestone Cleaning Projects." There you can learn more about the best ways to preserve and protect the gravestones of your ancestors for future centuries.

Photographing Tombstones

Myths and misconceptions abound about how best to document old tombstones in a way that does no harm to them. Genealogist and photo-historian Maureen Taylor published an article online at *www.genealogy.com/genealogy/64_gravestones.html* describing the hazards of gravestone rubbings and recommending photography as a safer alternative. Bright sunlight is a requirement, and you can improve the light quality by using a plastic full-length mirror to reflect the light upon the tombstone. You need a helper to position the mirror to highlight the stone's inscription while you take pictures. If you are using a digital camera, you can see the results immediately and adjust the positions of the mirror and camera accordingly.

Create a complete record of the graves by taking a series of pictures: shots of the whole cemetery, an image that includes the stones closest to your ancestors', a photo of the whole gravestone, and a picture in which the inscription fills the entire frame. Once you have some tombstone photographs, you may want to add them to the online Virtual Cemetery *(www.genealogy.com/vcem_welcome.html)* to create a memorial to your ancestors.

Unique Memorial Service

Beverly and Marcia Rice's ancestors were spiritualists during the California Gold Rush. Recently, their descendants arranged to have a reunion on the family farm, purchased in 1868, and to create a program of activities similar to what the ancestors might have done in their day. Using old photographs to help spot the exact locations, they served a meal on the old family picnic grounds, walked the same trails, and sat beside the same creek.

Moved by the spiritual atmosphere and ancestral traditions, the direct descendants decided to hold a séance to honor the beliefs of the mutual ancestors who had died and were buried there on the farm property. An experienced guide was invited to conduct the spiritual sharing session, and many of the participants were moved by the closer connections to both spiritualism and these ancestors.

Did your ancestors come through Ellis Island? You can now access the free online search service at *www.ellisisland.org*, where there are ship manifests (passenger lists) from 1892 to 1924. If you subscribe at a paid membership level, you can create a family scrapbook about your immigrant ancestors.

Ellis Island Immigration Center

In recent years, efforts to restore the Ellis Island Immigration Center in New York City have attracted widespread attention. None of my immediate ancestors actually came to America through Ellis Island, as it opened first in 1892, long after all my English family were already in America. My Canadian-born father arrived in Boston on the train.

But the desire of Americans to honor their immigrant ancestors and the appeal of this worthy endeavor inspired me—as a descendant of many immigrants—to purchase a nameplate tribute on the American Immigrant Wall of Honor at the American Family Immigration History Center, created by the Statue of Liberty–Ellis Island Foundation. I selected my maternal great-grandfather Charles Wardrobe to honor, as he was the last of my English ancestors to arrive, in 1863. The message on the certificate of registration (see Figure 13.2) applies to all our immigrant ancestors, from wherever and whenever they journeyed. You may want to consider this way of providing a lasting tribute to your immigrant ancestors.

Figure 13.2 Ellis Island certificate honoring an immigrant ancestor

Memory Books

Creating a memory book will be one of the most satisfying projects for the reunion. Since every family will want one, you might plan to include a memory book as part of each group's registration, or you can sell it separately.

Many people today enjoy an activity called "scrapbooking," which involves assembling a variety of information attractively into albums. You can find more information about scrapbooks at *scrapbooking.com* and *www.creativescrapbooking.com.* These handsome, cherished additions to an individual family's possessions are usually one-of-a-kind and not mass produced. For the reunion, you should create a memory book that can be easily duplicated and taken home by each family group so the memento can inform and entertain others for years to come.

The memory books I have created for the Wood family are placed in three-ring binders; the number of pages determines the size. "View binders" have clear overlays on the covers and spine to allow the insertion of personalized covers, like the one shown in Figure 13.3, and spine labels. I divide our memory books into five sections: Memories and Recollections, Famous Family Folks, Ancestry, Descendants, and English Origins.

Descendants of

Joseph and Anna (Palmer) Wood

Through Their Son
Capt. John and Persis (Hyde) Wood

Prepared for the Wood Family Reunion

July 30-31, 1994

Lebanon, New Hampshire

by   Sandra MacLean Clunies

DISCLAIMER: This is a compilation of research in progress, with much more data collection and verification required before formal publication. Contributions of additions and corrections, with sources and documentation, are most welcome.

Figure 13.3 Cover of the 1994 Wood memory book

"Memories" can cover any number of historical and sentimental recollections. Have you looked into old historic newspapers from your ancestors' home community during their lifetimes? Even if nothing in them specifically refers to your relatives, the advertisements, local news items, and other tidbits can tell you a lot about what life was like when your family lived there. The oral interviews described in Chapter 12 can be included in this section of your next memory book.

In the Memories and Recollections section, I place transcriptions from published town and county histories, data from military and pension records from the Revolutionary and Civil Wars, and some published sermons by two of our colonial-period family members. Someone had preserved a poem written for the 1936 reunion, and another deceased relative had written a talk on the family in the 1950s. At the end of her long life, my grandmother had recorded some of her life experiences as a child in the 1880s, which I also added to this section.

Famous Family Folks

Since both Joseph and Anna (Palmer) Wood had known ancestries back to 160 separate surnames in New England before 1650, our very ordinary family is shirttail kin to a lot of better-known people. Back in Chapter 1, the "cousin connections" chart (see Figure 1.3) shows relationships down to third cousins. Some of these "famous family folks" are actually sixth or seventh cousins to us, which makes them very distant relatives indeed. But everyone loves to be connected, however distantly, to both heroes and scoundrels from long ago, and I have researched links to more than seventy such famous or infamous personalities in American history.

Simple charts, such as the one shown in Figure 13.4, now show our relationships to several U.S. presidents; literary legends such as Louisa May Alcott, Emily Dickinson, and

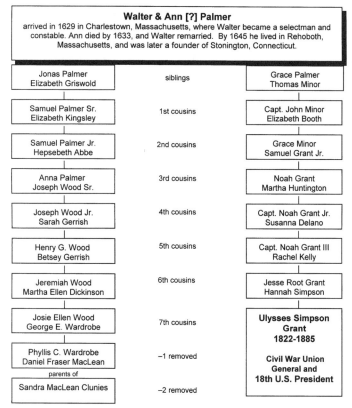

Figure 13.4 Chart showing that Wood family members are distant cousins to Ulysses S. Grant (Source: Gary Boyd Roberts, Comp., *Ancestors of America Presidents*, First Authoritative Edition [Santa Clarita, Calif.: Carl Boyer 3rd, 1995])

Ralph Waldo Emerson; military heroes such as Ethan Allen and Nathan Hale; inventors such as George Eastman and Eli Whitney; movie stars such as Katharine Hepburn and Anthony Perkins; and industrial pioneers such as F. W. Woolworth and W. K. Kellogg; as well as English links to Winston Churchill and Diana Spencer, Princess of Wales. Being a tenth cousin to a future king of England is not a very close relationship. Tens of thousands of living Americans share the same links, although most of us don't even know it. My family was fascinated to learn of their links to the worst serial murderer in American history in the 1890s and another to the last woman accused of witchcraft in 1692 Salem.

Some other common surnames have famous folks attached to them. A colorful and comprehensive Web site at *www.ericjames.org* serves as much more than just an extensive online repository for research on many James families. A focus of the site, shown in Figure 13.5, centers on the notorious western outlaw Jesse James and his infamous gang. A recent James family reunion honored an uncle of Jesse James, while the event cochair was Jesse's great-grandson.

Your family historians may not yet have found links to famous or infamous folks from history, but someone may have discovered the story of a few pioneer families or first immigrants to America. Collect and share these stories in the memory book. Even if your ancestors did not leave diaries, letters, or other personal memories of the past,

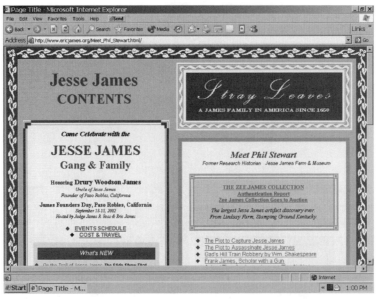

Figure 13.5 Honoring the uncle of the infamous Jesse James, at the James family Web site

you can simulate them by learning about their community at the time they lived there. Old newspapers, county and town histories, and other resources are available to fill in the blanks. Look for these in public libraries, genealogical societies, and state historical societies and archives.

Ancestries

Since our Wood family project aims to chart all descendants of one set of mutual ancestors, I include history sections on each of them. They lived in the late eighteenth century, but research has revealed their ancestry back to seventeenth century colonial New England, with a few lines going even farther back to England. As my data is computerized, I can print small charts on earlier generations of Joseph and Anna's ancestors.

I imported brief genealogical reports into the computer and added some simple charts at the top of each chapter to show the direct line of that surname to either Joseph or Anna (Palmer) Wood. I selected a few of the surnames from different geographical areas of the early colonies so I could show the families who were part of history in King Philip's War of the mid-1600s, the Salem Witch Trials of 1692, the Deerfield Massacre of 1704, the French and Indian Wars, and other historical moments in which these ordinary families had extraordinary experiences that should be remembered.

Heritage Help

Would you like to include photographs or maps of the family's ancestral villages in "the old country"? If you know the original hometowns of your immigrant ancestors, you can obtain photographs of the towns, countrysides, old cemeteries, and other places of interest, without leaving your living room. Go to *www.eurofocus.com* for countries in Europe or *www.pixelminers.com* for connections to countries all over the world (see Figure 13.6). Sites like these can also help you arrange future family tours to these heritage homelands.

Many families today arrange tours of the old country or connect with distant cousins still living there. I helped a family prepare for a visit to Europe to see where their ancestors had lived—a part of today's Germany called the Palatinate. I located an onsite genealogical researcher who was able to map out all the villages for their first visit. She found one particular house still standing that contained an ancestor's personal inscription high on a beam in the barn, dated 1834. The family has since taken the grandchildren along on a return visit to these villages and is now assembling a very

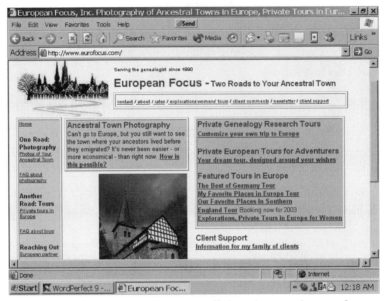

Figure 13.6 The European Focus site, offering photos and tours of ancestral towns

special memory book of their journey. The photographs include the American cousins dancing with their German cousins at a family party arranged just for the visitors.

Descendants

One section of my Wood memory book presents a fuller story of all the known descendants of the child of Joseph and Anna from whom the reunion guests descended. As my database already contains over a thousand descendants of Joseph and Anna and runs hundreds of pages, I chose to limit the section of the memory book to just the smaller group descended from one of their children. Each book was thus personalized. Staying with the color coding I'd used on the wall charts, the books that covered Joseph and Anna's son Luther had a green tab and the books on son Ephraim's line had a blue tab.

By keeping track of the reunion registration information, I knew about how many people were coming from each line. Each adult direct descendant over age eighteen received a personalized book. I figured that the older teens in a family would soon set out on their own and might want to have their own copy to take with them.

Family Origins

A scholarly study of the English origins of my Wood family was published in a respected journal in 1988, and I wrote the author for permission to photocopy the journal article for my reunion, permission she kindly granted. Filled with hundreds of citations and endnotes, it was *not* what you would call "easy reading," but it was the best record of our Wood family's earliest known history in print, and family members value it.

Check to see if some of your own family's early history has been researched and published by others. If you decide the material is reliable and credible, you might want to write to the author or publisher to obtain permission to duplicate it for your memory book.

There are many published resources to check out, both in print and online. One of the best is the Periodical Source Index (PERSI), an index to articles published in hundreds of journals, newsletters, and magazines produced by historical and genealogical societies. The Allen County Public Library in Fort Wayne, Indiana, maintains the PERSI, which now has almost two million entries indexed by topic, locality, and surname. PERSI is available on CD and online through Ancestry.com. If you're not a paid subscriber to Ancestry.com, check with your local library, where you may find access available to cardholders.

Find in-depth information on locating published resources about your family surnames in two other books in the NGS Series: *Genealogy 101* by Barbara Renick, and *Online Roots* by Pamela Boyer Porter, CGRS, CGL, and Amy Johnson Crow, CG.

Make It Your Own

The Wood family memory books have proven to be so popular that many reunion participants have asked for extra copies to take back to family members who were unable to attend. (An excerpt from one memory book appears in Figure 13.7.) After assembling nearly a hundred notebooks, involving many trips to the copy shop and hours of collating over one hundred pages for each book, I was not inclined to do it again so soon. So I cheerfully invited folks to trot down to their local copy shop and feel free to make as many copies as they chose.

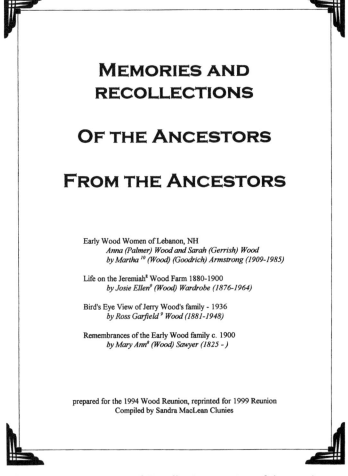

Figure 13.7 Memories and Recollections section of the 1994 Wood family memory book

Professional memory book publishers are available to help with your project. You can find some of these publishers online at *www.madmooncreations.com/fam.html* and *www.storypreservation.com/dp.html*. However, I believe you will find it more satisfying to gather a group of family helpers and create a memory book yourselves.

A memory book is a wonderful gift to provide, or sell for cost, to reunion goers. Check around the family now for those with the time, treasures, and willingness to take on this project. Perhaps a group can form a special team to gather materials, copy them, and assemble them into binders. It's a lot of work, but your memory book is truly a "labor of love." It honors your family in a most memorable way.

There are so many ways to pay tribute to your family's past: visiting historic family properties, restoring ancestral cemeteries, adding a name to the Ellis Island Immigration Center, creating memory books. The projects you plan will reflect the special features of your own family's history, and will be valued now and for generations to come. Now let's move on to the day you've been working toward and take a look at the last-minute details of your reunion.

CHAPTER 14

Opening Night (or Day)

IT'S ALMOST SHOW TIME! THE PRODUCER AND THE TEAM ARE GETTING a handle on all the last-minute details, you've sent your final reminder mailing (see Figure 14.1) to everyone expected to attend, and you're almost ready for the big day. Let's go over a few details here.

The Box Office: Registration

As people arrive for the reunion, signs should point them toward the registration desk—the welcome center and information center for the event. Have two or more trained volunteers sitting there to welcome folks, and have some of the senior production staff nearby to answer questions that arise during registration.

The business manager should have a copy of the record of deposits received and balances due, as well as paper invoices, at the registration desk. If you allowed attendees to order commemorative items like T-shirts, check to see whether a balance is due on those accounts. Of course, changes always happen: The Brown family paid deposits for three adult and two children's tickets and arrive to announce that fifteen-year-old Jennifer isn't with them. Is there a refund? If you have clearly communicated the refund policy, the answer is clear: "Sorry, we prepaid the caterer for her, and she ordered a T-shirt" or "We'll let you know once we tally the books after the reunion."

Plan to staff the registration desk throughout the first hours of the reunion because

1999 WOOD FAMILY REUNION

Descendants of Joseph[5] and Anna (Palmer) Wood
Original Grantees of Lebanon, NH 1766
July 30, 31, August 1, 1999

So Glad You're Coming to Join Us!

Here is our last reminder before the reunion. Enclosed is a map of the Lebanon area for you to find all the events.

BRING YOUR OLD PHOTOS & MEMORABILIA

We will have a computer and scanner set up to preserve all your old photographs for the 21st century. Please make a card with the names of all the people in each picture for our records. Scanning takes just a few moments and does no harm to the photograph, which will be returned to you within minutes. We will send you a scanned and printed copy after the reunion.

FRIDAY EVENING: Out-of-towners (or in-towners, too!) who want to join our Greeting-Meeting-Eating event should come to the Airport Economy Inn in West Lebanon *before* 7:00 P.M. Friday evening, July 30. From there, we will convoy to a nearby restaurant.

SATURDAY: We will begin at 10:00 A.M. at the Ski Lodge. (Helpers welcome to come at 9:00 to set up.) Lunch will be served at noon, and the group photograph and awards gathering will be at 2:00 P.M. Indoor and outdoor tables and activities for all. (Cleanup & take down 4:00-4:30.)

SUNDAY: Dutch-Treat Breakfast Buffet at 8:30 A.M. at the Radisson North Country Hotel. We have a special area set aside in the Atrium for the Wood Family Reunion party. The DAR Grave-Marking Ceremony for our mutual ancestor Joseph Wood will begin at 10:30 A.M. at Pine Tree Cemetery. Two separate tours of Wood properties in Lebanon and the Wood Farms of Kirby, Vermont, will leave from the cemetery about 11:30 A.M.

Until Wednesday evening, July 28, you can reach Sandy Clunies at *[my phone number]*
or by e-mail at *[my e-mail address]*.
Beginning Thursday evening, July 29, leave a message for her at the Airport Inn in West Lebanon.

Figure 14.1 Final reminder mailing

At the registration desk, have a cash box or zipped bag with small-denomination bills to make change, and make sure you issue receipts for cash payments.

people arrive at different times. If you expect a large crowd of relatives who won't recognize each other by face or name, consider having key staff wear something to identify them, such as a red cap, yellow sash, or reunion T-shirt.

At the registration desk, have a box or basket marked "Evaluation Forms," and ask every attendee to fill one out at the end of the event. You can learn a lot from your family's input and then use the suggestions when planning the next reunion. A sample evaluation form is shown in Figure 14.2. After registration, make this desk the "lost and found department." Clearly mark it so people know where to turn in and retrieve misplaced items.

Goodie Bags

A canvas bag with the reunion logo is an elegant idea for a goodie bag, but a costly one. At the Hatteras Homecoming, we used large plastic-handled bags to which we affixed a logo sticker of the event. For one Wood Reunion, I found a supplier of large plain brown paper bags with handles and put out a bunch of markers at the registration table. Then as each group signed in, we scooped up a set of "goodies" to put into a bag and urged the recipient to mark it with a name immediately.

The only drawback to my purchase of bags in bulk was that the minimum number was 250 and I needed only one hundred. Perhaps in your sleuthing for bags, you will find a supplier of reasonably priced sturdy bags in a smaller minimum order. Otherwise, as I did, you will have a grand supply of sturdy-handled bags to use or donate for later occasions.

A guest book becomes a permanent record for the archives. Make sure everyone signs in, including all children old enough to write. You are collecting signatures that will become a part of the future family archives.

Our Reunion Evaluation

Please help us plan for our next reunion
with your candid comments on this one.

	Great!	OK	Fair	Poor
Location	☐	☐	☐	☐
Food	☐	☐	☐	☐
Program	☐	☐	☐	☐
Publicity/Mailings	☐	☐	☐	☐

I most enjoyed _____

I least enjoyed _____

Suggestions for next time:

　　Location _____

　　Food service _____

　　Adult activities _____

　　Child activities _____

　　Other _____

　　_____

　　_____

(Optional) I can help next time with_____

(Optional) Name_____

Please drop this in the red bucket on the registration desk before you
leave—thanks!

Figure 14.2 Sample reunion evaluation form

At the registration desk, new arrivals will

- Receive a warm welcome
- Sign the guest book
- Pay any remaining balance
- Pick up their name badges
- Be handed a goodie bag that contains data update forms, small souvenirs, treats, the memory book, evaluation forms, maps, and so on.

The goodie bags should be strong; after all, the biggest and heaviest item you put in it could be the memory book. Other items you can include are imprinted ballpoint pens, coupons from local merchants, inexpensive stock sun visors, and small wrapped packages of peanuts and pretzels. Don't include such "hazardous materials" as chocolate candy, which will melt in the sun, or glass containers that can break if the bag is dropped. And be sure to leave room in the bags for the items folks purchase at Ye Olde Reunion Shoppe and for prizes they may win in the games and contests. Keep in mind that the community where your reunion takes place may offer tokens for your goodie bags; as you see in Figure 14.3, the New Orleans Multiculturalism Tourism Network offers to fill your goodie bags if you hold your reunion in that historic city.

Name Badges

Name badges facilitate mixing and mingling among all the families present. Adhesive and stick-on labels—those "Hello! My Name Is Bob" nametags—are less than useful, for they fall off many fabrics and cannot be attached to babies or small children who might be inspired to munch on them. So take time to plan this aspect of the reunion carefully and creatively.

Figures 14.4 and 14.5 show the name badge design I made for our last reunion. I prepared them on my computer without a special software program. Most word-processing programs have built-in label features that match almost any size of commercial labels or badges. Selecting a three-by-four-inch size, I created various templates to cover each of the seven lines into which we have divided the families. Note that on

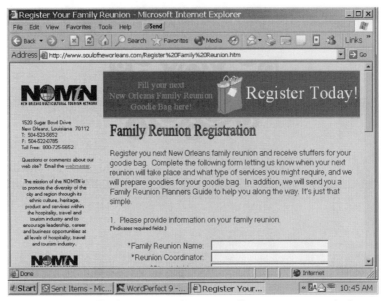

Figure 14.3 An offer from New Orleans to stuff your reunion goodie bags

the front side, the first name is enlarged for easy reading, followed by the surname, hometown, and whether the person is a direct descendant or an in-law. A colored adhesive sticker was added to each nametag to indicate the family line. Thus, all those with red stickers knew immediately that they all came down from Joseph Wood Jr. One of the signs posted in the hall summarized the colors and lines for easy reference.

On the reverse side of the nametag, note the abbreviated genealogy chart from the mutual ancestors down to the person wearing the tag (or a spouse as an in-law

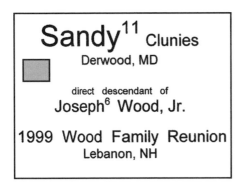

Figure 14.4 Name badge, front

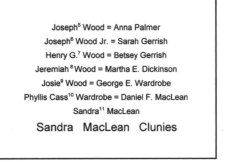

Figure 14.5 Name badge, back

descendant). This was easily accomplished by making templates of the common lines down for a few generations and then just adding the unique lines that led down to each particular attendee. Some genealogy software programs, such as Legacy at *www.legacyfamilytree.com/rptNameTags.asp,* can produce a different type of nametag with ancestors portrayed for three generations. But if you want to trace a line back for five, six, seven, or more generations on one badge, you'll have to make them yourself.

Wood reunion experience has proven that a soft elastic cord for holding the name badges, rather than pins or clips, is best. Clips were designed for men's suit jacket lapels—and you'll find few jackets and many T-shirts on reunion attendees. Pins can injure fabrics and small children. Budget-minded, I purchased a roll of soft elastic cord and attached them to the badges myself. But you can purchase name badge kits that include the cords at any large office supply store. Check *www.staples.com* or *www.officedepot.com* for price comparisons.

Computer Corner

The idea of using a scanner and laptop to digitize and present copies of old photographs and documents was presented in Chapter 11. Here are some other ideas to enhance the "computer corner" at your reunion site.

In addition to scanning old photographs and documents at the Hatteras Keepers Descendants Homecoming Event, I had the genealogy database of over 10,200 descendants of keepers on a laptop, and the printer allowed me to print charts for the descendants in seconds. I had also scanned actual signatures from the long-deceased keepers that I'd found in various public documents such as Civil War pensions and World War I draft registration cards, so I was able to provide a computer-generated copy of an ancestor's signature—a truly personal memento.

If you plan to have a computer corner, in addition to a computer, scanner, and printer, be prepared by having these items on hand: a three-prong adapter (older facilities may still have only two-prong electrical outlets), a surge strip, three-prong extension cords (in case the nearest outlet is too far away), velcro strips to tie up various connector cords and keep them safe from accidental disconnections, fresh batteries for all battery-operated devices, and (several) spare ink cartridges for the printer.

Before the reunion begins, connect and test all the components. At one reunion, I had brought along a new scanner and had not done a trial test of its compatibility with the laptop computer. Sure enough, just as soon as my son, the onsite expert, set up the equipment and greeted his first visitor—whose arms were full of unique old photos—the scanner would not play nicely with the computer. He spent an hour in frustrating attempts to fix the equipment and then had to go into town to the nearest computer dealer to solve the problem.

The team member operating the computer corner at your reunion doesn't have to sit there all day long. Announce times that the service will be open and available, and make sure the equipment is secured when unattended.

Prizes and Surprises

Chapter 9 emphasized the importance of having lots of prizes for contests and races. Other awards or prizes typical at a reunion recognize family members who meet special criteria, such as

- Person who traveled the longest distance to attend the reunion
- Person who traveled the shortest distance to attend the reunion
- Couple married the longest
- Couple married the shortest
- Family with the most generations present
- Oldest and youngest persons present

For these awards, you can use preprinted certificates—you will know the details from preregistration—or special reunion T-shirts. You should also add other categories that have special significance for your group. And add some amusing categories too, with inexpensive joke prizes you can purchase locally.

Surprises

It's fun to keep a few of the reunion details a secret or share them among as few planners as possible before the event. For instance, solicit an official proclamation or welcome letter on official letterhead issued by the local mayor, county council, governor, congressional representative, or other official, honoring your reunion and your family. This can be read aloud with great pomp and ceremony to the gathering. For such requests, most government offices appreciate notice of at least three months. Six months ahead wouldn't be too soon.

For suggestions on requesting a special proclamation, see the Web site of the governor of Nebraska at *gov.nol.org/Johanns/procs/proclamation.htm* and look at *www.denvergov.org/Mayor/395faq692.asp,* where the mayor of Denver gives similar guidelines.

Dress Rehearsal

For a Broadway show, it all comes together at the dress rehearsal, when the players are in costume, the sets are in place, and the orchestra replaces the tape player. The producers and directors sit in the audience to observe the action, note any last-minute changes, and put their stamp of approval on the whole production. For your family reunion, the week before the event is the dress rehearsal. You'll be making last-minute confirmations, having conversations with various reunion teams, and carrying around a clipboard full of lists so you can check off all the details. Now is the time for your last pre-event contact with a caterer or hotel to inform them of the final numbers of attendees, your last call to rental agencies to confirm that equipment orders will be ready on time, and your last-minute check of the dozens of other items on your list.

Figure 14.6 is the actual list I made for myself before heading north on a five-hundred-mile drive to the 1999 Wood Reunion. Despite this level of determination, I still forgot things and we had to improvise when the weekend event began.

Prepare the Understudies

The business world calls it "cross-training." The world of the theater calls it "understudying." Basically, it means that no single person is indispensable to achieving a goal. You have alternate people ready to step in should something happen to the prime person. These understudies need to be part of the planning and development process all along, so they're ready to substitute if needed.

Checklist of Stuff to Take to Wood Reunion

Saturday:

- [ ] Video of Bruce Wood & Daniel Wood
- [ ] 65 reunion memory books Brenda to carry them up in her car
- [ ] Rolls of charts, masking tape, double-stick poster tape, scissors
- [ ] 10 disposable cameras (name label on them to be returned)
- [ ] Bull horn, mic, speaker
- [ ] Laptop, scanner, zip drive, cables, surge strip
- [ ] Registration box: name tags, ribbons
- [ ] Roll of raffle tickets
- [ ] Box of large trash bags for cleanup (can leave there at 4:30)
- [ ] Two 3-fold display boards for Treasure Table

Sunday:

- [ ] Small flags
- [ ] Programs, biography booklets
- [ ] Appreciation certificates
- [ ] Blue cloth to "hide" marker before ceremony

Need to Get:

- [ ] VCR/TV (Roger checking)
- [ ] Put Sun. program and map in front cover
- [ ] Put descendant forms in each back cover to mail back
- [ ] Take checkbook
- [ ] Name tags inside notebook
- [ ] Later: large coffee can with cement, buried to hold marker
- [ ] Maps to Kirby

Figure 14.6 Last-minute checklist

One of the biggest burdens I have placed upon myself as producer of two major family reunions is not preparing enough understudies to assist. When my sister and I spent two solid hours at the registration desk and needed relief, we had plenty of volunteers who offered to help on the spot, but we had to pause and orient them to the task before we could stand up and move away: "Here's what you do with checks. Here's where the personalized memory books are located. Don't let anyone have one without checking off their name on this list over here." None of these important details were written down onsite—they were all in our heads. Next time, I will have written instructions for the registration desk so that anyone can help.

Expect the Unexpected

Remember, you cannot control the weather. That is a major fact for all who plan a reunion that includes outdoor events. Our 1994 Wood Reunion was held at a country club, where we had reserved a small building adjacent to the lakeside picnic area for registration and exhibits. The building contained two rooms, one of which had a few tables and chairs—not nearly enough to seat all the participants at one time— a restroom, and a small kitchen. As folks arrived, signs guided them into the building for registration and to see the exhibits we had placed in the front room. Then they moved outside to enjoy walks around the small lake, where clusters of chairs were set up to invite people to sit and chat while others were playing games, fishing, and swimming.

The morning was sunny and fair, and when the catering crew arrived to set up for lunch, a small canopy tent near the grills had some tables to hold the buffet dishes. Just as the aroma of grilled chicken and hamburgers wafted around the area, we felt the first undeniable gentle raindrops. The tent was not large enough to shelter all the diners, nor were the indoor rooms. So folks spread out in both places, while others stood under the shelter of the roof, and the dream of a "meal together" was rained out. Luckily, the showers soon ended and did not disrupt any later activities.

Medical Emergencies

Make sure that your reunion supplies include a small first-aid kit to handle minor bumps and bruises. If the Box Office remains staffed all day, the kit could be placed there as a central location. If a child is injured, find and let the parents supervise the response. Other medical problems may develop, especially with older people in attendance, so it's wise to prepare for them—and hope they don't occur. Have on hand this information:

- The names of people who have cellular phones with them
- Whether 911 connects to local emergency services
- The location and route to the nearest medical facility

Now that you have the supplies ready, all the players backstage, and the audience on its way, it's show time. The better prepared you are, the more likely you can join in on the fun with everyone else. So dim the lights, cue the orchestra, raise the curtain, and let the spotlight shine on your very own one-of-a-kind family reunion.

CHAPTER 15

The Curtain Falls

Postproduction Follow-up

IT'S NOT OVER WHEN IT'S OVER. THE CURTAIN HAS FALLEN, THE LAST bows have been taken, the fond farewells from the audience have faded into the sunset, and the reunion site is cleared of all evidence of the occasion. But there is still backstage work for the production team. Some of it immediately follows the show, such as getting all the leased or borrowed equipment back to the rightful owners. The records made at the reunion—the guest book, registration records, evaluations, oral and video interviews—must be carefully transferred from the event location to safe storage for later use. Other early postproduction efforts include money matters, thank-you letters, and evaluations.

Money Matters

It may be several weeks after the reunion, perhaps even several months, before the financial reports are completed. If team members are tardy in submitting their vouchers for reimbursement, a gentle nudge or announced deadline may be needed to speed that process along. Requests for refunds should be considered on an individual basis.

Once the business manager has completed the final reconciliation of income and expenses, a report should be generated telling you whether you broke even or had a shortfall or a surplus. The complete and detailed report becomes part of the reunion records you should save for the future. An abbreviated report can be included in the next newsletter to all the reunion participants.

193

If income did not equal expenses, consider asking for donations from your happy attendees to settle the account. If there is a surplus of income over expenses, you have a more enjoyable decision to make. Will you save a sum as "seed money" for the next reunion or to cover expenses for newsletters? Or will this fund some other project?

Thank You!

We all appreciate recognition and acknowledgment of our hard work, and your team deserves a lot of it. First, of course, you should acknowledge your many assistants during the reunion so they can bask in the group's applause. But now it's time to thank them again. A handwritten note of thanks is always appreciated. Certificates of appreciation are another nice touch. It's easy to make your own on a computer with a word-processing or publishing program. Personalize them by adding the reunion logo. Print them out on heavy-weight paper or card stock to mail off to all your hard-working production team members. Figure 15.1 offers a sample certificate of appreciation that you can use as the basis for your own.

Figure 15.1 Certificate of appreciation

Evaluations

We all learn from past experience, and your first reunion will guide you toward your next one. The evaluation forms you gave out at the registration desk are a good place to start. The production team should hold a post-show meeting to review the forms and to share conversations they had or overheard, in order to determine what worked well and what may need rethinking before the next show. You may even want to upload suggestions to the reunion Web site, as the Bray family did (see Figure 15.2).

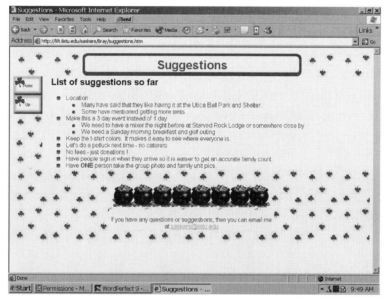

Figure 15.2 Planning ahead for the next Bray Family Reunion

In addition to requesting and reviewing evaluations from the reunion participants, it's also wise to listen to your various production teams—their thoughts and suggestions will also be critical to the success of the next reunion. Moreover, asking for their input in the post-reunion review validates the importance of their work. Some of the questions you should ask during your meeting, whether in person or by e-mail, might be

- Rate our timetables. Did we start early enough? What needs to be changed the next time?

- Rate our reunion site. Was it suitable? What could have been improved?

- Rate our communications. Did we confer often enough? Were we good support for each other? How could we improve?

- Rate our program and events. Which ones worked best? Least? Ideas?

- Rate our equipment and supplies. What did we forget?

Keeping in Touch

At reunions, friendships are renewed, new cousins are met, and people feel connected in a special way. Assure the crowd that keeping in touch is important—through newsletters, Web sites, e-mail, and chat groups, the same ways you contacted them in the first place.

Newsletters

In between our five-year Wood reunions, I send out at least one newsletter a year, usually at Christmas, that goes to everyone on my mailing list, including those who may also keep in touch via our family Web site. Figure 15.3 shows a sample from the newsletter I issued after our 1999 Reunion. While I may upload the same information to the Web, the "snail mailing" at first-class rates with "address correction requested" serves a second purpose: it lets me know if anyone has moved to a new address in the last year or two. Once forwarding services expire, the post office often returns a mailing with a notice of the address change, including a label with the new address.

Did you know you can upload a newsletter or flier and address list to the U.S. Postal Service Web site, pay online, and avoid all that printing and envelope stuffing, and all those trips to the mailbox? For details on this real time-saver, go to *www.usps.com/mailingonline/welcome.htm*.

Web Site

Many families duplicate their newsletters for a Web site or create electronic newsletters specifically for the online community—a time-saving and economical way to

WOOD FAMILY HOLIDAY 1999 NEWSLETTER

Descendants of Joseph & Anna (Palmer) Wood of Lebanon, NH

Editor: Sandy Clunies

Reunion 1999 . . . . . A Memorable Event !

Our last Wood Family Reunion of the 20th Century was surely a great one! Almost 150 people attended, and many of them for the first time.

We kicked it off on Friday evening with an informal gathering at the Economy Inn, after which many walked on down for a group dinner at a nearby restaurant.

By the time the first set-up team arrived at the ski lodge on Saturday morning, guests had already arrived, and the staff had yet to open the doors!

With unseasonably hot weather, and no indoor air-conditioning, it was a challenge to stay cool! But there were industrial-strength fans and we never ran out of ice ! Family charts were suspended from every wall and post, while albums of old photos were displayed. The plan to scan in photos was delayed while Sandy's son Jon struggled with "technical difficulties", but eventually everything worked and we saved dozens of wonderful photos of the family.

The catering staff of Endless Possibilities provided an elegant lunch, though none wanted to trade places with the staff hovering over the grills!

We honored Robert Leavitt, distant Wood cousin, and Lebanon's City Historian, with a gift of family charts. The raffle for the special American Flag flown over the US Capitol in honor of the Reunion was won by our senior member present, Alice (Ranney) McGinnis of VT, in her 90th year—one of the first to arrive and the last to leave Reunion '99 !

DAR Ceremony Honors Joseph Wood

On Sunday, many joined for the moving grave-marking ceremony at the Pine Tree Cemetery, which was conducted by members of the DAR, three of whom were Joseph Wood descendants. Family members also served as color guard, and provided vocal and instrumental music. A very talented family all around! Later on Sunday, some traveled up to VT's Northeast Kingdom to see the beautiful Wood farms there in Kirby - we loved the name of Virginia Wood's lovely property—Kinship Farm !

Stay in Touch For the 21st Century

Many family members who could not attend the Reunion in person have visited the Wood Family web site at MyFamily.com. This is one way to stay connected, and if others want to gain access to it, please let me know. I uploaded many photos from the Reunion, and there are dozens of antique photos and files there also.

Let me know of the events in your family— births, marriages, deaths. Once I finally reach federal retirement in February 2001, I can really get down to work producing that book on the family history !

Desc. of Jane (Wood) Colburn joined us for the 1st time this year !

Thanks to all of you who made so many contributions to the success of the 1999 Reunion. It was a privilege to coordinate it, and we shall work towards the first one of the 21st Century in 2004 !

Figure 15.3 Wood family holiday newsletter

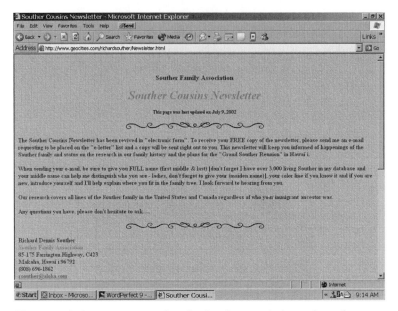

Figure 15.4 Announcement that the Souther cousins' newsletter has moved to an electronic format

keep your communications links current. If you do post an e-newsletter, you can print it out and send it by "snail mail" to those who do not have Web access. The Web has inspired some family newsletter editors to resume publication, as you can see in Figure 15.4, the announcement of the Souther cousins' publication.

Besides e-newsletters and uploading reunion photos, a family Web site offers many other creative uses. The Armer family encourages members to create their own personal Web pages on their site, as you see in Figure 15.5. This is a great way for the family to share news about each other and keep family alliances solid. Commercial sites such as *myfamily.com* allow your group to continue sharing information after the reunion ends.

Both commercial and individual family Web sites can have chat rooms so that, with passwords, two or more family members who are online can connect and "chat" with a degree of security—and save the cost of long-distance phone calls. Figures 15.6 and 15.7 show that our Wood family site at *myfamily.com* offers both e-mail and chat services, features that the Armer family also provides to its own members.

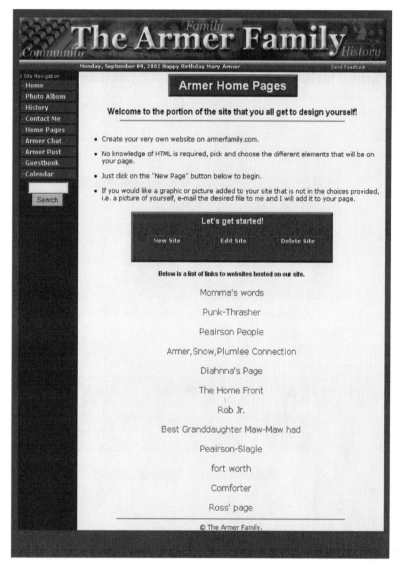

Figure 15.5 An invitation at the Armer family site to create your own individual Web page

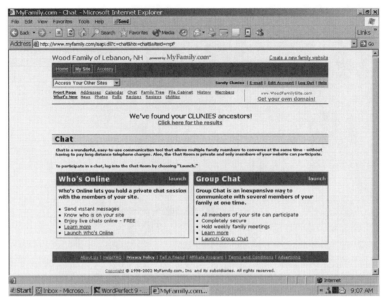

Figure 15.6 E-mail and chat services at the Wood family site at *myfamily.com*

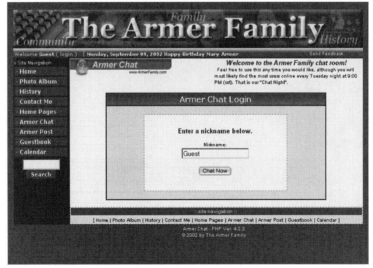

Figure 15.7 The chat room at the Armer family Web site

E-mail and Chat Groups

As I mentioned earlier, most e-mail programs allow you to create a "group" or "distribution list" that combines several selected individuals into one e-mail address. That way, you can create one message and send it to all those in the predetermined group. You may have set up a group for reunion planning; now you can set one up for a larger group of family members—and keep those messages flying.

In the 1950s, my mother and her nine siblings, plus their mother, began a round-robin letter that traveled from family to family across the country. After reading the package, you removed the letter you had written last and added a new one, and mailed it on. This letter continues today. We Hytrek cousins have also created our own electronic adaptation of the round-robin letter by setting up an e-mail list to trade family trivia and stay in touch.

—Bobbi King

Ongoing Projects

Another way to keep in touch is to create and develop ongoing projects that take place between formal family gatherings. In fact, the reunion is the perfect place to discuss the idea of special projects, some of which could even raise funds. If you developed a mission statement or statement of purpose, as suggested in Chapter 1, that statement may help you generate continuing projects.

Fund-raising for a Special Purpose

People are willing to give money for a good cause—and having a long-term fund-raiser can sustain interest and connection between reunions. How about establishing a family scholarship fund? Does an ancestral cemetery need restoration? Are you eligible to place a historic marker on a family property? Are there long-lost cousins back in the "old country" whom you would like to sponsor for a trip to America to attend the next reunion? Is there an old family property at which you could plant new trees as part of a future reunion event? Projects such as these require lots of planning and follow-up, so it's a good idea to ask attendees in advance about their interest in such activities. Unless you form a nonprofit association that receives IRS 501(c)(3) status, contributions to these accounts will likely not be tax-deductible. Ask advice from an accountant about setting up and maintaining such a group.

The Robey/Robie/Roby Family Association has become an active partner in a project to preserve an old country store in New Hampshire that was operated by family members for 110 years, and the Robie's Country Store Historic Preservation Corp. has obtained approval to be included on the National Register of Historic Places (see the announcement on the family Web site in Figure 15.8). The Family Association, which holds biannual reunions in various parts of the United States, plans to hold its 2004 Reunion in New Hampshire near the Robie Country Store.

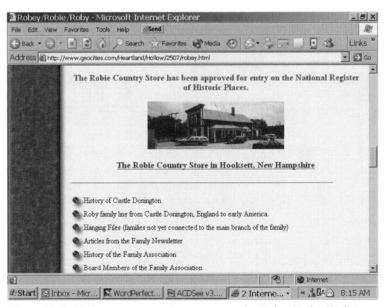

Figure 15.8 Update on an ongoing project at the Robey/Robie/Roby Association site

Reunion Videos

Creating a video of the reunion has many benefits. Not only is it available for those who attended to enjoy in the future, but it also provides a wonderful gift for those family members who were not able to be there, including those with frail health who could not travel. The videos can also be income producers. Perhaps you will just copy the "candid" version taken at the reunion and sell it "as is" to family members. This one will preserve all the spontaneous words and images, including Uncle Carl's reluctance to be photographed as he yells, "Get outta here with that thing!" But if your videographer did some editing or got professional help with the process and included titles, music, and still photos spliced into the visual production, your sale price should reflect that.

Some innovative families have placed a reunion video on their Web site for everyone to enjoy. Figure 15.9 shows members of the Hill-Raiford-Bullard families enjoying their reunion.

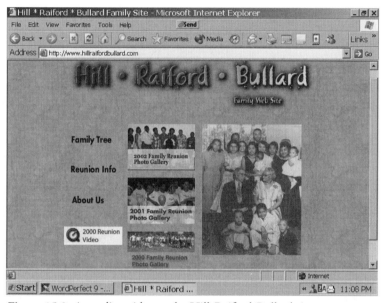

Figure 15.9 An online video at the Hill-Raiford-Bullard site

Family History Book

Besides the limited-edition memory book you may have offered at the reunion, there may be an interest in creating and publishing a larger family history book. Your family historian or genealogist should lead such a project, which may well take years to complete. In 1994 I told my family that I would have a book of all descendants of Joseph and Anna (Palmer) Wood ready by 1997. Guess what? It is still a "work in progress," and I have no idea when it will be done. *But I will complete it.*

Professional printing is expensive, especially for a relatively small number of copies (typically, a hundred copies of a family history book are published). You need to calculate whether sales will meet expenses. You may also want to look into whether a generous relative is willing to underwrite the project. I decided to go to a copy shop

You may choose to budget for an outside publisher to produce your family history book. You can find helpful resources online at *www.memorybooklets.com* and *www.photomemorybooks.com*. Also check out *www.cyndislist.com/books.htm;* scroll down to a section called Family History Publishers for references to companies that want to publish your book. But do consider creating this special book yourself, together with helpers in the family; you'll find it an inspiring and educational project.

when I wanted to compile what I did have on the Wood descendants, as my middle step in the plan to produce a full book. The pages were duplicated and put into a soft-cover spiral binding. Only thirty copies were produced, and five went to historical and genealogical libraries and societies.

You may also want to consider producing a history on CD-ROM. Figures 15.10 and 15.11 show announcements from the Robey and Dreisbach families about CD updates of their original histories.

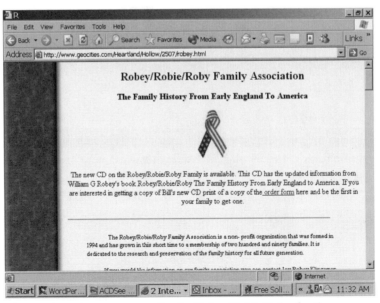

Figure 15.10 Announcement for the Robey/Robie/Roby family CD-ROM supplement

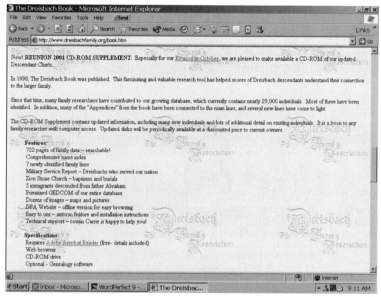

Figure 15.11 Announcement for the Dreisbach family CD-ROM supplement

Family Cookbook

Whether it's Cousin Helen's pickled herring, Aunt Minnie's ginger cookies, or Grammy's potato salad, a lingering legacy of your family's history is available to share with others—in a family cookbook. Select a skilled organizer (who need not be a gourmet cook) to coordinate the project. During the reunion, ask attendees to dig into those cherished old card files when they get home and extract their favorite recipes to share. While your goal is to preserve the best of the past, you should also survey the younger generations for some of their contributions, too. Gather up the recipes, sort them into categories, and add special touches like photos or other reminiscences of an occasion at which this dish was a featured highlight. Just input everything into the computer.

Want to have your cookbook printed by others? For samples of family cookbooks and a free publishing kit, go to Web sites such as *www.cookbookprinting.com* and *www.cookbookpublishers.com*.

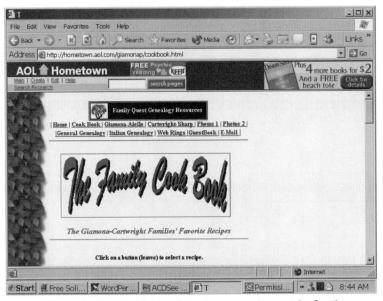

Figure 15.12 Online cookbook of the Giamona-Cartwright family

Once all the recipes, stories, and photos are collected, you can decide if you want to make a hard-copy book, an online e-book, or both. (For me, having a real book to have and to hold and to pass on to others is the way to go.)

Some families publish cookbooks to sell during and between reunions; many of these are attractive efforts, filled with stories and family photos. The Giamona-Cartwright families have created a space on a Web site to publish their electronic cookbook (see figure 15.12).

A successful reunion requires planning, creativity, and a healthy sense of humor. No event will be flawless. It is often those unplanned moments that turn out to be serendipitous, providing special memories that last a lifetime—and longer. As they enjoy the coming together of family members, all who attend your reunion will also better know and honor their ancestors and heritage. Your time spent planning and organizing this special occasion is your own gift of love.

Online Listings for State Parks

Note: The URLs lised here were valid at the time of publication. Another way to find a current site is to use a search engine and enter *"state park"* and the state's name.

Alabama
www.dcnr.state.al.us/parks/
state_parks_index_1a.html

Alaska
www.dnr.state.ak.us/parks

Arizona
www.pr.state.az.us/parksites.html

Arkansas
www.arkansasstateparks.com

California
www.parks.ca.gov/

Colorado
parks.state.co.us

Connecticut
www.friendsctstateparks.net

Delaware
www.destateparks.com/index.asp

Florida
www.dep.state.fl.us/parks/

Georgia
gastateparks.org

Hawaii
www.state.hi.us/dlnr/dsp/dsp.html

Idaho
www.idahoparks.org

Illinois
dnr.state.il.us/lands/landmgt/parks/

Indiana
www.in.gov/dnr/parklake/parks/

Iowa
www.state.ia.us/dnr/organize/ppd/

Kansas
www.kdwp.state.ks.us/parks/parks.html

Kentucky
www.state.ky.us/agencies/parks/

Louisiana
www.crt.state.la.us/crt/parks/

Maine
www.state.me.us/doc/parks/

Maryland
www.dnr.state.md.us/publiclands/

Massachusetts
www.state.ma.us/dem/forparks. htm

Michigan
www.michigan.gov/dnr

Minnesota
www.dnr.state.mn.us/state_parks/

Mississippi
www.mdwfp.com/parks.asp

Missouri
www.mostateparks.com

Montana
www.fwp.state.mt.us/parks/

Nebraska
www.ngpc.state.ne.us/parks/parks.html

Nevada
parks.nv.gov

New Hampshire
www.nhparks.state.nh.us

New Jersey
www.state.nj.us/dep/forestry/ parknj/divhome.htm

New Mexico
www.emnrd.state.nm.us/NMparks/

New York
nysparks.state.ny.us/parks

North Carolina
www.ils.unc.edu/parkproject/ncparks.html

North Dakota
www.state.nd.us/ndparks/

Ohio
www.dnr.state.oh.us/parks/

Oklahoma
www.touroklahoma.com

Oregon
www.prd.state.or.us

Pennsylvania
www.dcnr.state.pa.us/stateparks/

Rhode Island
www.riparks.com

South Carolina
www.discoversouthcarolina.com

South Dakota
www.state.sd.us/gfp/sdparks

Tennessee
www.state.tn.us/environment/parks/

Texas
www.tpwd.state.tx.us

Utah
parks.state.ut.us

Vermont
www.vtstateparks.com/htm/info.cfm

Virginia
www.dcr.state.va.us/parks/

Washington
www.parks.wa.gov

West Virginia
www.wvstateparks.com

Wisconsin
www.dnr.state.wi.us/org/land/parks/

Wyoming
spacr.state.wy.us/sphs/index1.htm

National Genealogical Society Standards and Guidelines

THE NATIONAL GENEALOGICAL SOCIETY HAS WRITTEN A SERIES OF genealogical standards and guidelines, designed to help you in your family history research. NGS developed these as a concise way to evaluate resources and skills, and serve as a reminder of the importance of reliable methods of gathering information and sharing it with others.

The NGS Standards and Guidelines appear on the following pages. They also appear online at *www.ngsgenealogy.org/comstandards.htm*.

Standards for Sound Genealogical Research
Recommended by the National Genealogical Society

Remembering always that they are engaged in a quest for truth, family-history researchers consistently

- Record the source for each item of information they collect
- Test every hypothesis or theory against credible evidence, and reject those that are not supported by the evidence
- Seek original records, or reproduced images of them when there is reasonable assurance they have not been altered, as the basis for their research conclusions
- Use compilations, communications, and published works, whether paper or electronic, primarily for their value as guides to locating the original records or as contributions to the critical analysis of the evidence discussed in them
- State something as a fact only when it is supported by convincing evidence, and identify the evidence when communicating the fact to others
- Limit with words like "probable" or "possible" any statement that is based on less than convincing evidence, and state the reasons for concluding that it is probable or possible
- Avoid misleading other researchers by either intentionally or carelessly distributing or publishing inaccurate information
- State carefully and honestly the results of their own research, and acknowledge all use of other researchers' work
- Recognize the collegial nature of genealogical research by making their work available to others through publication, or by placing copies in appropriate libraries or repositories, and by welcoming critical comment
- Consider with open minds new evidence or the comments of others on their work and the conclusions they have reached

Guidelines for Using Records, Repositories, and Libraries
Recommended by the National Genealogical Society

Recognizing that how they use unique original records and fragile publications will affect other users, both current and future, family history researchers habitually

- Are courteous to research facility personnel and other researchers, and respect the staff's other daily tasks, not expecting the records custodian to listen to their family histories nor provide constant or immediate attention
- Dress appropriately, converse with others in a low voice, and supervise children appropriately
- Do their homework in advance, know what is available and what they need, and avoid ever asking for "everything" on their ancestors
- Use only designated workspace areas and equipment, like readers and computers intended for patron use; respect off-limits areas; and ask for assistance if needed
- Treat original records at all times with great respect and work with only a few records at a time, recognizing that they are irreplaceable and that each user must help preserve them for future use
- Treat books with care, never forcing their spines, and handle photographs properly, preferably wearing archival gloves
- Never mark, mutilate, rearrange, relocate, or remove from the repository any original, printed, microform, or electronic document or artifact
- Use only procedures prescribed by the repository for noting corrections to any errors or omissions found in published works, never marking the work itself
- Keep note-taking paper or other objects from covering records or books, and avoid placing any pressure upon them, particularly with a pencil or pen
- Use only the method specifically designated for identifying records for duplication, avoiding use of paper clips, adhesive notes, or other means not approved by the facility
- Return volumes and files only to locations designated for that purpose
- Before departure, thank the records custodians for their courtesy in making the materials available
- Follow the rules of the records repository without protest, even if they have changed since a previous visit or differ from those of another facility

Standards for Use of Technology in Genealogical Research
Recommended by the National Genealogical Society

Mindful that computers are tools, genealogists take full responsibility for their work, and therefore they

- Learn the capabilities and limits of their equipment and software, and use them only when they are the most appropriate tools for a purpose
- Do not accept uncritically the ability of software to format, number, import, modify, check, chart or report their data, and therefore carefully evaluate any resulting product
- Treat compiled information from online sources or digital databases in the same way as other published sources—useful primarily as a guide to locating original records, but not as evidence for a conclusion or assertion
- Accept digital images or enhancements of an original record as a satisfactory substitute for the original only when there is reasonable assurance that the image accurately reproduces the unaltered original
- Cite sources for data obtained online or from digital media with the same care that is appropriate for sources on paper and other traditional media, and enter data into a digital database only when its source can remain associated with it
- Always cite the sources for information or data posted online or sent to others, naming the author of a digital file as its immediate source, while crediting original sources cited within the file
- Preserve the integrity of their own databases by evaluating the reliability of downloaded data before incorporating it into their own files
- Provide, whenever they alter data received in digital form, a description of the change that will accompany the altered data whenever it is shared with others
- Actively oppose the proliferation of error, rumor, and fraud by personally verifying or correcting information, or noting it as unverified, before passing it on to others
- Treat people online as courteously and civilly as they would treat them face-to-face, not separated by networks and anonymity
- Accept that technology has not changed the principles of genealogical research, only some of the procedures

Standards for Sharing Information with Others
Recommended by the National Genealogical Society

Conscious of the fact that sharing information or data with others, whether through speech, documents or electronic media, is essential to family history research and that it needs continuing support and encouragement, responsible family historians consistently

- Respect the restrictions on sharing information that arise from the rights of another as an author, originator or compiler; as a living private person; or as a party to a mutual agreement

- Observe meticulously the legal rights of copyright owners, copying or distributing any part of their works only with their permission, or to the limited extent specifically allowed under the law's "fair use" exceptions

- Identify the sources for all ideas, information, and data from others, and the form in which they were received, recognizing that the unattributed use of another's intellectual work is plagiarism

- Respect the authorship rights of senders of letters, electronic mail, and data files, forwarding or disseminating them further only with the sender's permission

- Inform people who provide information about their families as to the ways it may be used, observing any conditions they impose and respecting any reservations they may express regarding the use of particular items

- Require some evidence of consent before assuming that living people are agreeable to further sharing of information about themselves

- Convey personal identifying information about living people—like age, home address, occupation, or activities—only in ways that those concerned have expressly agreed to

- Recognize that legal rights of privacy may limit the extent to which information from publicly available sources may be further used, disseminated, or published

- Communicate no information to others that is known to be false, or without making reasonable efforts to determine its truth, particularly information that may be derogatory

- Are sensitive to the hurt that revelations of criminal, immoral, bizarre, or irresponsible behavior may bring to family members

Guidelines for Publishing Web Pages on the Internet
Recommended by the National Genealogical Society

Appreciating that publishing information through Internet Web sites and Web pages shares many similarities with print publishing, considerate family historians

- Apply a title identifying both the entire Web site and the particular group of related pages, similar to a book-and-chapter designation, placing it both at the top of each Web browser window using the <TITLE> HTML tag, and in the body of the document, on the opening home or title page, and on any index pages
- Explain the purposes and objectives of their Web sites, placing the explanation near the top of the title page or including a link from that page to a special page about the reason for the site
- Display a footer at the bottom of each Web page that contains the Web site title, page title, author's name, author's contact information, date of last revision, and a copyright statement
- Provide complete contact information, including at a minimum a name and e-mail address, and preferably some means for long-term contact, like a postal address
- Assist visitors by providing on each page navigational links that lead visitors to other important pages on the Web site, or return them to the home page
- Adhere to the NGS "Standards for Sharing Information with Others" (see page 213) regarding copyright, attribution, privacy, and the sharing of sensitive information
- Include unambiguous source citations for the research data provided on the site, and if not complete descriptions, offering full citations upon request
- Label photographic and scanned images within the graphic itself, with fuller explanation if required in text adjacent to the graphic
- Identify transcribed, extracted, or abstracted data as such, and provide appropriate source citations
- Include identifying dates and locations when providing information about specific surnames or individuals
- Respect the rights of others who do not wish information about themselves to be published, referenced, or linked on a Web site
- Provide Web site access to all potential visitors by avoiding enhanced technical capabilities that may not be available to all users, remembering that not all computers are created equal
- Avoid using features that distract from the productive use of the Web site, like ones that reduce legibility, strain the eyes, dazzle the vision, or otherwise detract from the visitor's ability to easily read, study, comprehend, or print the online publication
- Maintain their online publications at frequent intervals, changing the content to keep the information current, the links valid, and the Web site in good working order
- Preserve and archive for future researchers their online publications and communications that have lasting value, using both electronic and paper duplication

Guidelines for Genealogical Self-Improvement and Growth
Recommended by the National Genealogical Society

Faced with ever-growing expectations for genealogical accuracy and reliability, family historians concerned with improving their abilities will on a regular basis

- Study comprehensive texts and narrower-focus articles and recordings covering genealogical methods in general and the historical background and sources available for areas of particular research interest, or to which their research findings have led them
- Interact with other genealogists and historians in person or electronically, mentoring or learning as appropriate to their relative experience levels, and through the shared experience contributing to the genealogical growth of all concerned
- Subscribe to and read regularly at least two genealogical journals that list a number of contributing or consulting editors, or editorial board or committee members, and that require their authors to respond to a critical review of each article before it is published
- Participate in workshops, discussion groups, institutes, conferences and other structured learning opportunities whenever possible
- Recognize their limitations, undertaking research in new areas or using new technology only after they master any additional knowledge and skill needed and understand how to apply it to the new subject matter or technology
- Analyze critically at least quarterly the reported research findings of another family historian, for whatever lessons may be gleaned through the process
- Join and participate actively in genealogical societies covering countries, localities, and topics where they have research interests, as well as the localities where they reside, increasing the resources available both to themselves and to future researchers
- Review recently published basic texts to renew their understanding of genealogical fundamentals as currently expressed and applied
- Examine and revise their own earlier research in the light of what they have learned through self-improvement activities, as a means for applying their new-found knowledge and for improving the quality of their work-product

Glossary

Americans with Disabilities Act (ADA): The law that requires public facilities and services to provide access to all persons regardless of physical limitations and special needs.

Ancestor: A person from whom you are descended.

Audio/visual equipment: Microphones, speakers, tape recorders, lighting, cameras, screens, projectors, and related supplies.

CD drive: A device on a computer that reads compact discs.

Census: An official count of a population.

Certified Genealogist (CG): A credential issued by the Board for Certification of Genealogists (BCG) to persons who have demonstrated specific skills and knowledge in conducting family history research.

Collateral relationships: Those connections among close and distant cousins to a mutual ancestor.

DAR: See **Daughters of the American Revolution.**

Database: Any collection of specific information from index cards to computerized programs.

Daughters of the American Revolution (DAR): A membership society of women who can prove a direct relationship to an ancestor who provided support for the American Revolution from 1775 to 1783.

Demographics: The characteristics of human populations that may identify or define a particular audience or market, such as sex, age, or geographical location.

Download: To transfer data from one computer to another, usually from a remote larger mainframe computer on the Internet to a personal computer.

E-mail: Electronic mail or messages passed from one computer to another.

Emigrants: Persons leaving their home country to relocate to another.

Emigration: The process of leaving one's homeland for a new country.

Family association: An organization of persons interested in researching the same family.

Fixed expenses: Those reunion costs, such as facility rent, that remain constant regardless of the number of people who attend.

Genealogy wall charts: Computer-generated or hand-drawn charts to illustrate relationships among generations of individuals in a family.

Immigrants: Persons who arrive in a new country from another homeland.

Immigration: The process of arriving in a new country from another homeland.

Informant: A person who provides information.

Internet: A system of computer networks that includes the World Wide Web, as well as other dimensions.

Mail list: A discussion group conducted online to which users subscribe.

Message board: An online community gathering place where you can post a message, respond to someone's request for information, or learn more about a topic; also known as a *bulletin board* or a *forum.*

Metasearch engine: A search engine that looks within other search engines and provides results from many sources.

Multigenerational event: a gathering at which persons of all ages can participate together.

Proclamation: An official document issued by a mayor, governor, or other official to honor a special event.

Query: A research question you send, by mail or e-mail, to others who may have information you need.

SASE: See **Self-addressed stamped envelope.**

Scanned image: The result of using a scanner to transfer a photograph, illustration, or document to an electronic format that can be sent to other computers.

Search engine: A tool used on the Internet to seek specific information from a variety of Web sites.

Self-addressed stamped envelope (SASE): Literally that, an addressed, stamped envelope included in a letter or mailing to encourage a response from the recipient.

Siblings: Brothers and sisters, all children of the same two parents.

Social Security Death Index: A database maintained by the federal government that lists persons who died during the time they were collecting Social Security benefits.

Spreadsheet: A computer program format that organizes information for easy sorting and retrieval.

Upload: To transfer data from one computer to another, usually from a personal computer to a larger remote mainframe computer on the Internet.

URL: Uniform Resource Locator—a unique Internet address used to access a Web site.

Videographer: The operator of a video camera.

Web: See **World Wide Web.**

World Wide Web: Part of the Internet that provides access to commercial and personal Web sites.

ZIP drive: A storage device that can be internal or external to a computer.

Index

National
Genealogical
Society

. . . . the national society for generations past, present, and future

What Is the National Genealogical Society?

FOUNDED IN 1903, THE NATIONAL GENEALOGICAL SOCIETY IS A dynamic and growing association of individuals and other groups from all over the country—and the world—that share a love of genealogy. Whether you're a beginner, a professional, or somewhere in between, NGS can assist you in your research into the past.

The United States is a rich melting pot of ethnic diversity that includes countless personal histories just waiting to be discovered. NGS can be your portal to this pursuit with its premier annual conference and its ever-growing selection of how-to materials, books and publications, educational offerings, and member services.

NGS has something for everyone—we invite you to join us. Your membership in NGS will help you gain more enjoyment from your hobby or professional pursuits, and will place you within a long-established group of genealogists that came together a hundred years ago to promote excellence in genealogy.

To learn more about the society, visit us online at *www.ngsgenealogy.org*.

Other Books in the NGS Series

Genealogy 101

Barbara Renick

A guide to basic principles of family research, this is a book the uninitiated can understand and the experienced will appreciate.

$19.99
ISBN 1-4016-0019-0

Online Roots

Pamela Boyer Porter, CGRS, CGL

Amy Johnson Crow, CG

A practical guide to making your online search more effective and creative. Includes how to know if what you find is accurate and the best way to make full use of the Internet.

$19.99
ISBN 1-4016-0021-2

Planting Your Family Tree Online

Cyndi Howells, creator of Cyndi's List

How to create your own family history Web site, share information, and meet others who are part of your family's history and heritage.

$19.99
ISBN 1-4016-0022-0
Coming Soon